DISCOVER YOUR KID'S
SPIRITUAL GIFTS

Many have told me—and I have told many others—that repentance is good for the soul. This means that I am now ready to repent for excluding children from my teaching and practice on spiritual gifts. Adam Stadtmiller has convinced me that we also need to draw children into the full picture of equipping the whole body of Christ to discover, develop and use their spiritual gifts. This is a groundbreaking book!

C. Peter Wagner
Author of *Your Spiritual Gifts Can Help Your Church Grow*

Spiritual gifts are not just for adults only! Helping our children discover and use their God-given spiritual gifts may just be one of the most important roles of any Christian parent. I'm convinced that kids who learn to serve within their spiritual gifts will stay centered on God. Adam Stadtmiller's spiritual gift assessment tool is a great opportunity for parents and youth workers to have life-changing faith conversations with their kids.

Jim Burns
President of HomeWord
Author of *Faith Conversations for Families* and *10 Building Blocks for a Solid Family*

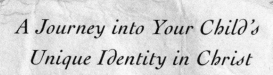

A Journey into Your Child's
Unique Identity in Christ

DISCOVER YOUR KID'S SPIRITUAL GIFTS

ADAM STADTMILLER

Regal

From Gospel Light
Ventura, California, U.S.A.

Published by Regal
From Gospel Light
Ventura, California, U.S.A.
www.regalbooks.com
Printed in the U.S.A.

Library of Congress Cataloging-in-Publication Data
Stadtmiller, Adam.
Discover your kid's spiritual gifts : a journey into your child's unique identity in Christ /
Adam Stadtmiller.
p. cm.
ISBN 978-0-8307-5956-9 (trade paper)
1. Gifts, Spiritual. 2. Christian children—Religious life. 3. Christian education—Home
training. I. Title.
BT767.3.S72 2012
234'.13083—dc23
2011031539

Rights for publishing this book outside the U.S.A. or in non-English languages are
administered by Gospel Light Worldwide, an international not-for-profit ministry.
For additional information, please visit www.glww.org, email info@glww.org, or write
to Gospel Light Worldwide, 1957 Eastman Avenue, Ventura, CA 93003, U.S.A.

To order copies of this book and other Regal products in bulk quantities,
please contact us at 1-800-446-7735.

In 1989, Dave Chrysler took on the task of discipling a raw, fresh off drugs, lover of Jesus. Much of what you read in this book was shaped during our weekly times together in Dave's kitchen. I can honestly say that I learned as much from this mechanic and discipler of men as I ever did in seminary. This book is dedicated to him.

Contents

FOREWORD

The countdown screen flashed 4 minutes and 59 seconds until start time. The heavy bass music pounded in cadence with the countdown numbers on the giant screen. Hundreds of kids bumped into each other and talked a steady stream as they filed through the doors and found their places in the sanctuary. My son Jordan wished he'd stayed home. He simply didn't feel up to attending youth group that night.

Six months prior to that night, Jordan took a late hit in football, which seriously injured his back. He could barely walk. He couldn't carry even one of his schoolbooks. He wore a stiff brace and needed extra time to shuffle from one class to another. The last six months had devastated all of us. We went from one doctor to another, one treatment to another, but to no avail. Jordan's severely herniated disc pressed on three sets of nerves and would likely require back surgery. He was only 17 years old. I'd heard stories of 30-year-old men with this same injury, and who, even though they had the surgery, ended up on disability, requiring their wives to be the breadwinners of the family.

We watched a big part of Jordan disappear somewhere deep inside him as he watched the lives of his friends go on without him. Attending youth group was a heroic feat for him because of the pressing crowds, the call to sit down and stand up, and because everyone around him seemed happy and able to move freely.

But this youth group was a special place to be. Jordan needed reminding that God was on the move and loves to work through His people, no matter what age, season or stage of life they are currently walking through. These kids were constantly mobilized and challenged to step up, to position themselves to be used by God. That particular night the youth pastor asked a young student to share about his experience on a recent mission trip.

With his hands in his pockets, the young man stood awkwardly on stage. He shrugged his shoulders, grabbed the microphone, titled his head and said, "Yeah, so, I used to think that God no longer healed people but, uh, then I went on this mission trip. Well, this little child was sick and I prayed for him, and, uh, well, God healed him. So yeah, I guess God still heals today." He shrugged again and then simply walked offstage.

At that moment my son's heart pounded out of his chest, and the Lord whispered to him, "I want you to ask that boy to pray for you after service tonight." Jordan knew God was speaking directly to Him. The youth pastor took the stage and preached his message. The worship team followed as students came forward for prayer. Jordan—my shy, reserved son—pressed through the crowds (which was so unlike him) and looked for the non-descript student who spoke earlier that evening.

Jordan approached the student, stuck out his hand and said, "I'm Jordan Larson. I have a bad back injury. Wondering if you'd pray for me." Once again the boy shrugged his shoulders and said, "Yeah, sure." He put his hand on the small of Jordan's back and prayed. Jordan felt a little heat but nothing more. However, once he got out to the parking lot he noticed something. No pain. He titled from left to right. Nothing. He reached down to touch his thighs. No pain. He bent over forcefully to touch his knees, then his toes, and then he took off sprinting through the parking lot!

God healed Jordan that night! He showed up to train with the football team the very next morning. For six months the players and coaches watched Jordan shuffle through life. That morning when they asked him what happened, with a captive audience before him, he simply said, "God healed me last night."

Now, I'll admit, I don't fully understand God's ways regarding healing. I'm still waiting for Him to heal me. But I do believe that we'd see more evidence of God's power and provision in our day if more of us dared to walk in faith. And isn't it something how God used a young student who, though he didn't exactly comprehend God's willingness to intervene, stepped out and made himself available anyway? And look what God did! Our lives will never be the same!

That's why I'm so excited about the book you now hold in your hands. Adam has skillfully crafted an encouraging and practical guide to help parents (and youth workers) equip and mobilize children to be the hands and feet of Christ in a world so desperately in need. In this book, Adam shares that our gifts have a tendency to either flourish or wither depending on our stewardship of them. So true!

Scripture tells us that the *same power* that raised Christ from the dead is available to us, at work in us. Do we believe that our children have a lesser version of that same power? Or will we lay hold of the very real opportunity to train our children to walk in their spiritual gifts so they might see God's power activated in their lives?

I've had a number of guests on my show to discuss the alarming percentage of college kids abandoning their faith once they leave their Christian homes. Across the board the experts have assessed that though glitz, fog machines and video games may get young kids in the door, they won't keep them in the faith. Of the young people who stay committed to their spiritual roots, these are the two common denominators: they were taught the Word of God in their growing up years, and they were given opportunities to serve others by using their spiritual gifts.

I believe this book is an important word for our times, and it has released at just the right time. Read it. Soak it in. You'll not only be awakened to the wonder of how God longs to work through your child, but you'll also be challenged afresh to look for Him in your own life. And, as a quick side note, no matter where you stand theologically on some of the spiritual gifts listed in Scripture, you'll appreciate that Adam navigated through that territory with great balance, respect and honor.

May God bless you as you read.

Susie Larson
Host of *Live the Promise*
Author of *Growing Grateful Kids*

ACKNOWLEDGMENTS

A big thanks to my wife, Karie, and our girls, Lily and Lucy, who put up with me during these projects. You are God's blessing to me.

Blessings to the Regal/Gospel Light team. It's is amazing to partner with a group of people so committed to seeing kids thrive in their relationship with God. I also want to acknowledge all of the parents and kids who either directly contributed to this book or helped me refine the spiritual gift assessment. Many of them you will meet as you read through these pages.

Gracias also to Dan Fields. You are an amazing photographer. I love your ministry of images (http://danfieldsphotography.com).

IMPORTANT NOTE

Before you begin reading chapter 1, take a moment to complete the Spiritual Gifts Assessment for your child(ren) beginning on page 143. This will provide you with questions that the text of the book will answer. You will then do the assessment again after reading the book.

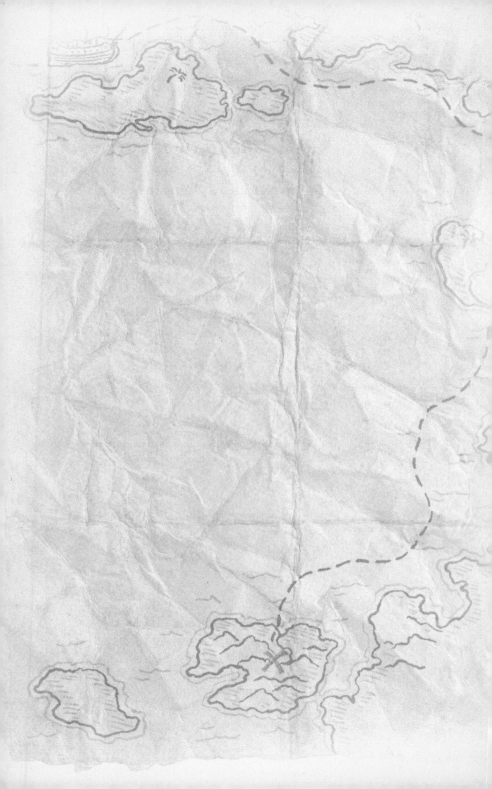

PART ONE

A Case for Spiritually Gifted Kids

*Ever since I was about nine, I have had a passion for little kids.
I absolutely love the way they light up at the glimpse of something
as simple as a cookie. I love the way they love Jesus.*

*I have always wanted to see a clear purpose in my life. I used to ask
my mom what I was good at. I longed to be like other kids and be
good at sports, art or playing an instrument. So when my mom
would tell me that I was good with kids, of course my response was,
"That doesn't count." It wasn't until a few summers ago when
I started to believe that it really did count.*

*I worked in my church nursery watching kids almost every Sunday
night for five years, but it wasn't until the summer of 2010 that
I really found my place. There is a program that Forest Home
Family Camp runs called the Childcare Assistant Program for girls
aged 13 to 18. Here, girls like myself pay for the opportunity to
come, be discipled and work with the children of parents who bring
their kids to summer family camp. The program gives me an
opportunity to grow in my faith and in my giftings.*

*Understanding my spiritual gifts is something that I struggled
with regularly. I have now found something that I love and that
glorifies God at the same time. Because God has blessed me with the
incredible skills needed to work with kids, I am most certainly going
to use them to please Him. Being passionate about children as well
as helping them figure out their lives in Christ makes me want to
have a future working with kids. Recognizing your spiritual gifts is
the hard part, but the easy part is using them for the glory of God.*

Madison, Age 15
Our Family's Child Care Assistant at
Forest Home Family Camp,
Summer 2011

How Christian Can a Kid Be?

A Case for Spiritual Gifts in Kids

But there I have another name. You must learn to know me by that name. This was the very reason why you were brought to Narnia, that by knowing me here for a little, you may know me better there.

ASLAN TO EUSTACE, LUCY AND EDMUND

I believe kids have spiritual gifts.[1]

It all started right before our daughter Lily's fourth birthday. We were at Disneyland again. We have season passes, so we go about once a month. If you know Disneyland, you know that in order to get to the Pooh and Tigger hang-time area, you have to pass by Splash Mountain.

Splash Mountain is your classic logjam attraction. It's an incredibly slow and monotonous floating journey full of campy, mechanized characters. The payoff for the drudgery of this ride is the chute. Here, the log you are riding in drops into the abyss for 2.7 seconds of sheer terror.

Thus, it surprised me when, as we were heading toward the land of honey pots and tailless donkeys, Lily stopped, fascinated by the screaming people descending into the chute, and exclaimed, "I want to go on that, Daddy!"

At first I tried to talk her out of it. I didn't think she was old enough. Surely, I misunderstood. Persistent, Lily insisted she wanted to ride Splash Mountain. Thankfully, I knew attractions like these had height limits. Three-year-olds don't belong on thrill rides. At some point, Lily would be turned back by some sensible Disney cast member, and we could get back to more appropriate childish pursuits.

So, off we went to find out what I already knew. As we walked through the entrance to the ride, I noticed there were no height charts. It seemed that anyone could board as long as he or she had an accompanying adult.

Not knowing if I had made a huge mistake by allowing Lily to make this decision, we boarded our log. I prepared myself for six minutes of terrified toddler, begging me to go back; but there would be no going back, we were committed. This was bad parenting. Lily would be emotionally scarred for life.

How Christian Can a Kid Be?

I'm not sure when or why it happened, but somewhere back in the Church's grand history, we decided that only certain elements of a full life in Christ are available to our kids. This is definitely true in regard to spiritual gifts in kids. At some point, someone put up a spiritual height chart, and generations of Christian kids have been missing out on the ride of their lives ever since!

> I'm not sure when or why it happened, but somewhere back in the Church's grand history, we decided that only certain elements of a full life in Christ are available to our kids.

Our spiritual gifts are like a thrill ride of faith, and they are one of the most dynamic ways we come to know Christ and mature in our relationship with Him. When we walk in our spiritual gifts, we get our hands and feet dirty for Jesus, and we start to look and act like the Christians of the Bible.

Relegated to the Teen Years

If there is one place where we, as a church of Christian parents, are hindering our children, it is in not believing that our kids, even very young kids, can walk powerfully according to the Spirit and in the spiritual gifts bestowed on them.

In Luke 18, we see that even the disciples themselves were prone to marginalizing children to a role of spiritual bystander rather then seeing them as Kingdom-bringing collaborators in the faith.

Christ's disciples felt that children should be near Jesus but never experience Him deeply, sit on His lap, pull His beard, melt in His embrace or gaze deeply into His eyes.

> People were also bringing babies to Jesus to have him touch them. When the disciples saw this, they rebuked them. But Jesus called the children to him and said, "Let the little children come to me, and do not hinder them, for the kingdom of God belongs to such as these. I tell you the truth, anyone who will not receive the kingdom of God like a little child will never enter it" (Luke 18:15-17).

Part of the power of this teaching is found in the verses that follow this passage. There we find a devout man who knew all about God and had followed all the rules since he was a boy; but when Jesus tested his faith with devotion that goes beyond a law of strictly knowledge, he fell away. This is what happens when a child's spiritual upbringing focuses solely on knowing truth rather than intertwining truth with experience.

> A certain ruler asked him, "Good teacher, what must I do to inherit eternal life?"
>
> "Why do you call me good?" Jesus answered. "No one is good—except God alone. You know the commandments:

'Do not commit adultery, do not murder, do not steal, do not give false testimony, honor your father and mother.' "

"All these I have kept since I was a boy," he said.

When Jesus heard this, he said to him, "You still lack one thing. Sell everything you have and give to the poor, and you will have treasure in heaven. Then come, follow me."

When he heard this, he became very sad, because he was a man of great wealth (Luke 18:18-23).

One thing that we must understand going forward is that God desires that we offer the whole faith to our kids, not just the bits we think they can assimilate. This means that, like us, our kids have a calling to minister now!

I don't know why we have relegated the dynamic fullness of Christian living to the teen years and beyond. It is like we spend the first 10 to 12 years of a child's life telling them all about God, but never letting them actually explore the reaches and riches of knowing God in active ministry for themselves.

Perhaps we have camped on the words of Proverbs 22:6, believing that protecting our kids from the wiles of the world and filling them with Scripture and truth is the road to creating a sustainable faith. This can often be a fear-based model of provision and protectionism rather than an equipping faith-based one:

Train a child in the way he should go, and when he is old he will not turn from it.

What many parents have misunderstood is that the training model the original Hebrew author was referring to is a hands-on Deuteronomy 6 discipleship. This is the style Jesus used. It is the kind of training and discipleship that happens in the trenches of ministry rather then in clean and tidy synagogues and churches.

Love the LORD your God with all your heart and with all your soul and with all your strength. These commandments

that I give you today are to be upon your hearts. Impress
them on your children. Talk about them when you sit at
home and when you walk along the road, when you lie
down and when you get up. Tie them as symbols on your
hands and bind them on your foreheads. Write them on the
doorframes of your houses and on your gates (Deut. 6:5-9).

This kind of discipleship training only happens when we partner with our kids in the unique ministry God has called them to.
This is why exploring and releasing our kids into their individual
spiritual gifts and ministry is of utmost importance. Our spiritual
gifts act as a playing field of belief and faith. Spiritual gifts equal
ministry, no matter what the age.

When this does not happen, it is very possible that like the
man in Luke 18, our parenting style will fashion kids who know all
about God but have never experienced Jesus in a heart-changing
way. These are the kids whose faith often goes into remission on
reaching the magical age of 18. These are kids who have knowledge but not the Davidic intimacy we see in the psalms.

Give Your Kids the Entirety of the Gospel

The entirety of the gospel and all of its intention is meant for children as well as adults. When the Holy Spirit came in power, it was
for the empowerment of the entire church. The fullness, power
and gifts of the Spirit were distributed in a new way. The Kingdom
was now open to all. The veil had been torn. The power of God was
no longer confined to a handful of prophets, priests and judges.
The playing field was extended, and all were invited to participate.
No one who believes on the name of Jesus has been left out.

In Ephesians 3, the apostle Paul makes it clear that the fullness of Christ is available to the entire family of believers. This includes your kids. As you read this Scripture passage, see if your
understanding of the richness of the Christian life you expect for
your children matches up to this passage's intent. If not, ask yourself why not?

For this reason I kneel before the Father, from whom his whole family in heaven and on earth derives its name. I pray that out of his glorious riches he may strengthen you with power through his Spirit in your inner being, so that Christ may dwell in your hearts through faith. And I pray that you, being rooted and established in love, may have power, together with all the saints, to grasp how wide and long and high and deep is the love of Christ, and to know this love that surpasses knowledge—that you may be filled to the measure of all the fullness of God. Now to him who is able to do immeasurably more than all we ask or imagine, according to his power that is at work within us, to him be glory in the church and in Christ Jesus throughout all generations, for ever and ever! Amen (Eph. 3:14-21).

Equipping the Entire Body

The book of Acts is all about equipping believers in Jesus for Kingdom ministry. This equipping was one of power and practicality. Like steroids in an athlete's body, the indwelling power of the Holy Spirit was now empowering all those who believed to do greater works for the Kingdom than they could ever have done before.

Kids don't have to graduate from junior high or high school before they can dramatically impact their world and culture for Jesus. Believing kids are called to not only understand the faith but also, like us, to find their unique ministry and purpose, and live it out to the fullest. Navigating this journey with them is part of our divine commission as parents.

Kids—your kids—have the ability to evangelize and share the truth of God in a way that can bring even the most stoic atheist to his or her knees. Kids, even small kids, can pray and see others healed. Children, when led by the Holy Spirit, can speak knowledge and wisdom beyond their years. They are encouragers, servants and givers.

From the days of John the Baptist until now, the kingdom
of heaven has been forcefully advancing, and forceful men
lay hold of it (Matt. 11:12).

Children can rip God's kingdom from the sky and release it
with a vibrant infusion into this dull and sullen world. That is, if
we as adults do not hinder them with our unbelief.

> Children can rip God's kingdom from the
> sky and release it with a vibrant infusion into
> this dull and sullen world. That is, if we as
> adults do not hinder them with our unbelief.

Spiritual Gifts Establish Kids in Him

One of the reasons I am still following God today, and ultimately
went into vocational ministry, is because I was under a pastor who
immediately got me walking in my giftings at the time I recom-
mitted my life to Jesus. Pastor Dave knew there was staying power
in God's gifts. I was definitely not ready; it had only been a month
since I had stopped using drugs and alcohol. It had only been 30
days since my friend Torry had pulled me out of a Tijuana gutter.
Nonetheless, Pastor Dave asked me to help him lead a small-group
Bible study.

I balked when Dave asked me to help in this task. *Really? He
wanted me to co-lead a Bible study? No way, pal, I'll just sit back and take
it in.* Dave was persistent. He would not let me off the hook. So,
with my cigarettes still hidden in the glove compartment of my
car—it would be awhile before I got free of that habit—I dove into
God's Word.

Pastor Dave's belief in me, and insight into my spiritual gifts,
created a magnetic pull that connected me to Christ. Immediately,
I went from being a bystander to an active participant in the faith.
I loved preparing for the Bible study each week. Under the covering

of Pastor Dave, I came alive. I fell in love with God's Word. I fell in love with God.

The same is true for our kids. When they experience God in their giftings, they will be established in their faith. They will begin to create a history of experiences in which God has backed up their faith with His manifested presence. Your kids will know that they are Christian in more than title only. They will know it in their bones. This is because when we step out in faith, and into our gifts, we challenge God to show up. If you have ever walked in your giftings and seen God move, you know what I mean.

> As you therefore have received Christ Jesus the Lord, so walk in Him, rooted and built up in Him and *established* in the faith, as you have been taught, abounding in it with thanksgiving (Col. 2:6-7, *NKJV,* emphasis added).

If someone can give me a good argument why spiritual gifts are not available to kids, I would like to hear it. Like you, I want to walk in the truth of God's Word, not some fabrication of my imagination. With that said, I don't believe you will be able to disprove my understanding. Instead, if you begin to help your child discover more of God in his or her personal spiritual gifts, you will find that your child will begin to know God in a deeper way! When we step out in faith, and into our gifts, we challenge God to show up.

When we step out in faith, and into our gifts, we challenge God to show up.

Playground Missionaries

Over the last four years, I have been a playground dad. This is because we feel that God has called our family to the public school system. Every Friday at 12:45 P.M., you will find me at Lily's school. It's my favorite part of the week.

When Lily entered kindergarten, my wife, Karie, and I believed the best way to make an impact on her campus was to be a consistent presence while recruiting as many other believing parents to do the same.

While I definitely believe God is using Karie and me to help create a Kingdom-bringing difference on that school campus, we have become converted to the idea that we are only a second line of support, a backup if you will. What we have come to understand is that if Lily's campus is to be truly transformed for Jesus, it is going to have to happen through Lily and her believing friends. The most influential missionaries Christ will ever send to your kids' school are your kids!

Since gaining this realization, we have gone from primarily trying to gather other parents to Lily's campus to discipling Lily to assemble and minister alongside her friends.

Believing that Jesus can create a campus revival through the very kids who traverse the halls and playground on a regular basis is a basic Christian premise. God uses His people, all of His people, to change the environments and cultures they encounter on a daily basis.

> But thanks be to God, who always leads us in triumphal procession in Christ and through us spreads everywhere the fragrance of the knowledge of him (2 Cor. 2:14).

The Spiritual Gift of Intercession/Prayer, Blacktop Style

Recently, I got to experience God using Lily and her gifts for the purpose of reaching her school for Christ. One night, when tucking Lily into bed, the Lord prompted me to ask her if she had been using her gift of intercession/prayer. (As we move on through this book, I will share how you can determine your children's spiritual gifts.)

Lily's answer blew me away. This is what she said: "Well, today I decided not to play at recess and instead walked around the campus to pray for the kids and teachers at my school." Excuse me? Did I hear that right? Lily had taken initiative and decided to "prayer walk" her campus while sacrificing her playtime?

If that is shocking to you, let me assure you that it was shocking for Karie and me as well. We had never talked to Lily about intercession on that level. All we had really done was encourage her to pray for her friends each night before she fell asleep.

On my bed I remember you; I think of you through the watches of the night (Ps. 63:6).

I'm embarrassed to say that this could have been another time when we hindered Lily in her faith if the Holy Spirit had not led her around the hindrance. We had confined Lily's intercession to her bedroom, never dreaming that a child would give up recess to seek God for her friends and teachers. Thankfully, the Holy Spirit had more expansive plans.

Aslan and Child Spirituality

As I close this chapter, I want to turn your attention toward Narnia. In C. S. Lewis's books, the Chronicles of Narnia, we find an author who believed that kids were more than spectators to the faith. At the conclusion of *The Voyage of the Dawn Treader*, Aslan talks to Peter, Lucy and Eustace about this crucial season of life and how it would set their course for the future:

"Please, Aslan," said Lucy. "Before we go, will you tell us when we can come back to Narnia again? Please. And oh, do, do, do make it soon."

"Dearest," said Aslan very gently, "you and your brother will never come back to Narnia."

"Oh, Aslan!!" said Edmund and Lucy both together in despairing voices.

"You are too old, children," said Aslan, "and you must begin to come close to your own world now."

On the shores of Narnia, we are faced with something every parent already knows. One day our children will grow up, the constant questioning will cease, childlike faith will be challenged by adult reason, and our children will be one step closer to knowing.

In the Narnia series, C. S. Lewis elegantly portrays this brief period of childhood spirituality. Lewis presents the spiritual walk of children as a captivating time when kids are not considered vases to be filled, but fires to be lit.[2] These are kings and queens, children who fight real spiritual battles, have their faith tested, and walk in their individual gifts for the glory of Aslan's kingdom.

"Are you there too [in adulthood and back in the real world], Sir?" said Edmund.

"I am," said Aslan. "But there I have another name. You must learn to know me by that name. This was the very reason why you were brought to Narnia, that by knowing me here for a little, you may know me better there."[3]

This final statement illustrates why I have written this book. It is because I believe that we must seize the opportunity to disciple our kids into their spiritual gifts; that by knowing Jesus, "here for a little" might translate into creating in them a glorious lifetime of following Jesus.

Shooting the Chute

When Lily and I reached the chute at Splash Mountain, I was nervous. Then something happened that I never expected. Instead of crying and holding on for dear life, Lily lifted her arms into the air and screamed for joy as we dropped off what seemed like the face of the earth. Lily was unabashedly sinking her teeth into life and loving every minute.

I see those moments as some of the most memorable of my parenting experience. God took 2.7 seconds and gave me an eternal understanding. Our kids are not looking to be spectators, but rather to be thrilling, Kingdom-bringing participants in this life we know as Christ!

Notes
   1. This applies to believing children of any age. Spiritual gifts are only granted to believers.
   2. This is adapted from a quote by François Rabelais (c. 1494–1553), a French renaissance writer.
   3. C. S. Lewis, *The Voyage of the Dawn Treader* (New York: MacMillan, 1988), p. 209.

Bumblebees and
Spiritual Gifts

Providing a Platform for Spiritual Gifts

*I was really proud of myself. I thought that this was an adult thing—
that only adults could do; but kids could do it as well.*

MISHA LOTTO, FIFTH-GRADE SCIENTIST

So what do bumblebees have to do with spiritual gifts? The answer is a whole lot if you are looking for an example of young people's ability to live beyond the boundaries often set for them.

Last year, a small elementary school science project gained international acclaim when a group of third- and fourth-graders discovered something about the way bumblebees pollinate that scientists had failed to see before.

The experiment was set up by one of the children's parents. Dr. Beau Lotto, a neuroscientist, volunteered his time, but it was the children who did the research. The study dealt with the way bumblebees choose the individual flowers they forage from.

The first thing the kids did was to create a bee habitat. This Plexiglas box was divided into quarters and prepared with a matrix of colorful dots that made up a contextual puzzle. Each dot's center was filled with sugar water so that there would be consistency in the study.

What the experiment found was that bees deploy different strategies when it comes to decision-making. Some bees went straight for the bright dot in the middle of each circle. Other bees touched many areas outside the center of each dot before choosing the flower to pilfer.

Before this point, scientists had believed that bees made these decisions based solely on color. The other assumption was that all bees made their choices in the same way. This groundbreaking study has created an avalanche of new research, and its findings were published in a major scientific journal.[1]

When Dr. Lotto was asked about how the kids were able to come up with such a dramatic discovery, he said it came down to three simple steps. The first was, and these were his words, [they had] "access to stuff." In this case, it was the raw material to make a bee habitat. The next was, "confidence." The kids needed to know that they were asking questions that mattered—questions that other people cared about. Finally, the class needed a platform to share what they had learned.[2] If you think about it, this is pretty much the exact strategy Jesus used when raising up His disciples.

When Dr. Lotto's son, Misha, was asked about how he felt after having his study published in *Biology Letters*,[3] he said the following: "I was really proud of myself. I thought that this was an adult thing, that only adults could do, but kids could do it as well." When pressed about what this meant for the young boy's life, he replied that he had decided to become a scientist like his father.

Kids Respond to Challenge

What this story illustrates is that kids respond to challenge. Children and teens are looking for someone to help them ask the right questions and then provide a framework for them to experiment. In the words of Dr. Lotto, they need someone to give them not only "access to stuff" but also the confidence to implement what they discover. In Misha's case, it was a scientific father who took time away from his important career to build a bee habitat with some kids.

When parents do things like this, they are speaking the language of children. They are saying, "You matter, and I believe in you. Let's go explore this great big world together and discover where we fit." As we journey further into the concept of your child's unique spiritual gifts mix, I want to do so with an eye on the above story. In it you will see an easily replicable pattern when creating a context of spiritual discovery for your kids.

The Process for Releasing Your Kids into Their Gifts

1. *Give them access to stuff:* Discover and train them up in their personal spiritual giftings.
2. *Provide confidence:* Let your kids know you believe in them and their abilities for God. Encouragement is an incredible equipper!
3. *Provide a platform:* Find ministry opportunities that match their giftings and partner with your kids in those ministries.

I love it that Dr. Lotto used the phrase "access to stuff." You would expect a professional scientist to use some impressive word to describe the criteria and substance needed for this important study. Instead, Dr. Lotto used the word "stuff." For our kids, words like "stuff" demystify big concepts like spiritual gifts. Your parenting genius will be displayed as you practice the art of explaining and releasing your kids into the depths and "stuff" of God in a way that they can access.

One of the other things I want to acknowledge is that the concept of children's spiritual gifts is foreign to most parents. As I said earlier, many mothers and fathers have no idea where they fit into the Body of Christ, let alone where their children fit. One of the reasons Misha was able to succeed as a scientist was because he had a father he was able to emulate. Dr. Beau Lotto was not just a scientist in title. He did not just wear a white coat around the house. Beau was a real scientist who engaged in legitimate experiments and discoveries. Beau Lotto is the real deal.

> Your parenting genius will be displayed
> as you practice the art of explaining and
> releasing your kids into the depths and "stuff"
> of God in a way that they can access.

Below is a recent email Karie and I received from our good friends Andrew and Jennifer. I asked Andrew and Jennifer to send me their thoughts on spiritual giftings because I knew they were aware of these within the lives of their kids and were developing strategies to help their kids grow in their giftings. I also know that hearing from other parents can be a huge encouragement. Here is what they wrote:

Hey Adam, I wrote out some of the thoughts I've had over the last few weeks regarding your request. It was a great reminder to keep on building my kids up in this way.

I think it can be overwhelming for a parent to set out to discover his kids' spiritual gifting. Depending on your own comfort level with the idea of spiritual gifts, this can seem like an arduous task.

The first time I thought about my role in helping our kids discover their spiritual gifts was only after I began to look at who it was that God made me to be. I remember being asked to serve in the children's ministry for three-year-olds. I thought, *No problem, easy. I love kids.* But I [Jennifer] was surprised at how little I enjoyed it. After all, I'm a mom. I love kids. And yet I found myself, every week, watching the clock, counting the minutes for church service to be over.

One week, someone didn't show up for their shift for children's ministry check-in. I was asked to fill in. This is where I began to love serving. I had a deep desire to wel-

come people when they came in the door. I naturally grav-
itated to those parents who were new and a bit confused as
to where to go. I know that dropping your kids off in a
new environment can be uncomfortable. I wanted to let
them feel secure with who would be caring for their kids.
I remembered how I felt as a first-time visitor, completely
lost and unsure.

Continuing in the check-in ministry, I made friends
with the families and remembered many of the kids'
names week after week. This is where I soared. This is what
I loved. Because I was serving out of my gifts of service,
hospitality and mercy, it didn't seem like work at all. It was
what God made me to do. I often stayed at that greeting
post the entire service, well beyond my shift.

When parents like Andrew and Jennifer know who they are in
Christ and what their own spiritual gifts are, they will naturally
find it much easier to lead their children in their gift. When this is
not the case, it can be like trying to teach a child to swim when
you can't swim yourself. The rest of Jennifer's email shows us what
happened after she grasped who she was created to be in Christ:

With this fresh realization, I began to look at my kids' spiritual gifting in a new way. Who has God made them to be?
What is in their spiritual DNA? What do they specifically
have to bring to the Kingdom? I discovered that the church
finds its fullness and life when believers serve in their God-
inspired uniqueness.

I started off by encouraging my kids in the gifts that I
saw them bring to the table. To my eldest son, Josh, I
would say, "From a young age people have always seen the
LORD in you. You have an ability to hear and discern from
the LORD, just as I do." To Nate I would say, "You have
such a heart for worship."[4] I said this because I observed
Nate respond to the worship we played in the car and at
home. This led Nate to pursue teaching himself the guitar

and leading worship in the two-year-old class. With Abby, we wanted to affirm her pastoral gifting.[5] As often as possible, we would highlight what we saw in her with words like, "You are so nurturing. Have you noticed how much younger children love you?"

What Jennifer and Andrew did here is so fundamental in building up kids in the faith. It is also the second rule of encouraging children, according to Dr. Lotto's bee experiment. That rule is confidence. The ability to recognize and then encourage your children is atomic in nature. It builds upon itself. Encouragement breeds confidence. Confidence when under the authority of the Holy Spirit is called faith. According to Scripture, we are not able to live in God without it.

We live by faith, not by sight (2 Cor. 5:7).

This is often the tipping point of spirituality. The day we know who we are in Christ and have the confidence of faith to step out is the day that our life with God becomes dynamic. It is the day the adventure really begins. I am sure that you have experienced this with your child. Not long after you first got her (or him) in the pool, you put her on the tile cornice and encouraged her to jump. Eventually, with your encouragement, she jumped off the ledge and into your arms. Before long, she was asking you to judge the distance of her farthest solo jumps into the deep end. It is the same with our children's spiritual steps and their ability to experience ever-greater adventures with God!

Jennifer finishes her email by giving us an example of the third step in releasing our kids into their spiritual gifts. Jennifer recognized a platform for ministry and partnered with her kids in it.

After we began to understand our children's spiritual makeup, we began to look for opportunities for our kids to put their gifts into practice—to be in ministry. I remember a very elderly lady coming to our garage sale one day. I recognized her from around town and asked her how she was. She proceeded to tell me about a recent fall that had left her in constant pain for several weeks. My sons were both standing by. I knew that my son Josh in particular loved praying for others. I asked the lady if we could pray for her. The frail woman accepted with urgency. Right there, in the middle of the garage sale, with people milling all around us, I asked Nate to get her a chair. My two sons and I laid hands on the woman and prayed for her healing. She thanked us with tears in her eyes, obviously touched. I never saw that woman again, but I can't help thinking of my sons that day and how that opportunity to pray for this woman without hesitation or embarrassment changed their spiritual lives.

Like you, Andrew and Jennifer are normal parents. They have all of the foibles and struggles of the rest of us. They don't hold degrees in spiritual parenting. What they do have is a hunger and thirst for God, combined with a desire to see their children have the same. Both of these traits are available in infinite measure to all who would aspire to walk in them.

You're Already an Expert

Trust me, you already know the process of identifying your child's spiritual gifts. Sure, you might not know what all the individual gifts are yet, but you know how to identify and go after the things you want for your kids. Here's what I mean. One of our desires is to have both of our girls be proficient snowboarders and skiers. While Karie and I are not professional riders by any stretch of the imagination, we are excellent at helping our girls become very competent at these sports. Both Lily and Lucy began riding when they were two years old. While Lucy is still in the "fetal" stages of her career, her eight-year-old sister, Lily, has not met a black diamond run she didn't like.

Lily and Lucy are becoming proficient snowboarders because Karie and I had a desire for them to become proficient. We know what a good snowboarder looks like. We know when a snowboarder's turns are not up to par and when they are not getting enough speed for the flat sections up ahead. Besides knowing how to teach them about the intricacies of snowboarding, we also have geared our lives around this pursuit. Much of our discretionary vacation time and finances are focused on making sure that Lily and Lucy have every opportunity to excel at snowboarding and skiing.

You have a similar story with your child. Maybe you are not snowboarders, but I am sure there is something else that you have desired for or recognized in your child that you are helping him or her pursue. Whether it is dance, football, the arts or academics, you know how to direct your child to experience and gain proficiency in these things. You are dedicated to doing these things. Think about it. How much do you drive your kids around to practice? How much have you spent on lessons? How many times have you thrown the ball in the backyard with your kid, making sure that he or she has a proper follow-through?

You can see where I am going with this. Once you know what the spiritual gifts of intercession/prayer, evangelism or hospitality look like, and you get excited about them, the sooner you can apply what you already know to these areas. So let's get started!

Notes

1. "Children's Bee Study Makes It to Royal Society Journal," BBC News, Education and Family, December 22, 2010. http://www.bbc.co.uk/news/education-12058868.
2. "Elementary School Project Gets Published," PRI's The World, December 24, 2010. http://www.theworld.org/?s=beau+lotto.
3. See Biology Letters at http://rsbl.royalsocietypublishing.org.
4. While I did not add worship to my list of spiritual gifts, I believe a scriptural case can be made for this gifting. See 1 Samuel 16:23; Psalm 34:3; 1 Chronicles 9:33; 2 Chronicles 5:12-14.
5. A pastoral gifting does not mean that you are going to be in full-time vocational ministry. The Holy Spirit, for the purpose of caring for God's flock, often distributes the pastoral gift to those who are not called to full-time vocational ministry.

Summer Camp, Emotional Scars and Spiritual Gifts

What Is Essential?

One man considers one day more sacred than another; another man considers every day alike. Each one should be fully convinced in his own mind. He who regards one day as special, does so to the Lord.

THE APOSTLE PAUL ON CHRISTIAN
LIBERTY IN NONESSENTIALS
(ROMANS 14:5-6)

When I was five years old, my parents got the great idea to let my brother and me go to summer camp. Within a couple of days of my graduation from kindergarten, we packed up the Commander motor home and began the long drive from San Diego to Camp Kennolyn, a camp in the mountains above Santa Cruz, California.

Besides the emotional angst and ensuing "scars" that resulted from being dropped off for two weeks, at the age of five, with a bunch of strangers all wearing the same forest green T-shirts, it was a pretty cool camp. Actually, Camp Kennolyn was more like Disneyland than a camp. It had all the bells and whistles. It was probably more opulent than I would send my kids to, but who is to say those fencing and dressage lessons won't pay off someday?

The kind of summer camp you send or don't send your kid to says a lot about what you value as a parent. Do you want your kids to rough it, or be pampered in the Bahamas? Are horses on the agenda, or water sports? Maybe you are all about a missions experience, or family camp. Whatever it is, it says something about you.

Your view on spiritual gifts also puts you in a camp. You might not know it, but what you believe about spiritual gifts will let others know what you value.

Since the devil knows this, he has used spiritual gifts as a key battleground to divide Christians for centuries. Arguments about what gifts are available today or how many gifts should be considered true spiritual gifts have torn apart many a work of God.

The apostle Paul did his best to defuse the tension involving gifts by putting them in the non-eternal category. By non-eternal, I mean the things that will have no further significance in heaven. Take a look:

> Love never fails. But where there are prophecies, they will cease; where there are tongues, they will be stilled; where there is knowledge, it will pass away. For we know in part and we prophesy in part, but when perfection comes, the imperfect disappears. When I was a child, I talked like a child, I thought like a child, I reasoned like a child. When I became a man, I put childish ways behind me. Now we see but a poor reflection as in a mirror; then we shall see face to face. Now I know in part; then I shall know fully, even as I am fully known. And now these three remain: faith, hope and love. But the greatest of these is love (1 Cor. 13:8-13).

Paul, in 1 Corinthians 13, makes it very clear that spiritual gifts are a passing and imperfect thing. Yes, Paul knew how important spiritual gifts are to the kingdom work of the Father, but he also knew that they are not in the same category as the theological absolutes of Jesus' virgin birth or justification of our sins by faith.

In the end, your personal or denominational stance on the gifts won't matter. What you did and how you acted in love through the pouring out of your life through your spiritual gifts will. What I mean by this is that the gift will pass away, but the results of that gift will last forever.

Branding

Like you, the brand or group of spiritual gifts I espouse are what I believe to be true and supported by Scripture. These views have been backed up by many personal experiences that I will share as you continue to read. With that said, I am always aware that, as Paul warns, we only see in part (see 1 Cor. 13:9).

Here's my point: Unlike the eternal truths, such as Christ's work on the cross or the doctrine of the virgin birth, I'm just not willing to die or divide the Body of Christ for the non-eternal elements of Scripture. This includes my personal and denominational view of spiritual gifts. As believers, we should show liberty and grace in regard to the gifts. This is especially true given the fact that the Church is evenly divided between those who believe all of the original gifts are available for today's believers and those who don't.

> One man considers one day more sacred than another; another man considers every day alike. Each one should be fully convinced in his own mind. He who regards one day as special, does so to the Lord. He who eats meat, eats to the Lord, for he gives thanks to God; and he who abstains, does so to the Lord and gives thanks to God. For none of us lives to himself alone and none of us dies to himself alone. If we live, we live to the Lord; and if we die, we die to the Lord. So, whether we live or die, we belong to the Lord (Rom. 14:5-8).

To be completely honest with you, the primary reason I wrote this book was so that you would have the tools to release your kids into ministry. I know that sounds weird, but I did not set out to be a spiritual gifts guru, nor do I want to be one unless it translates to changed lives and a changed world for Jesus. What I really care about are kids being released into ministry and falling in love with Jesus, to the depths of their hearts and for the long run. This happens when they get their hands dirty for Jesus. Stepping out in their spiritual giftings is one of the best ways for this to happen, and for your kids' lives to be transformed!

If you find a gift or two you don't want to add to your personal cache of available gifts, let it go. This is especially true if it goes against your church's stance on spiritual giftings. We are only called to exercise the gifts in accordance to the measure of our faith. With that said, I hope that as you turn the rest of these pages, you will be better equipped to help your child take his or her place and God-given position among the redeemed.

> We have different gifts, according to the grace given us. If a man's gift is prophesying, let him use it in proportion to his faith (Rom. 12:6).

Available Gifts

How many of the spiritual gifts listed in Scripture are available to us today? This is one of the most hotly contested debates in the Church today. As a matter of fact, this dispute has been going on for about 2,000 years.

On one side of the discussion we have those who believe that some of the gifts were only temporary and for the launching of the Church. On the other side of the aisle we have those who ascribe to the belief that all of the gifts are in play today. Since I am writing to the whole Church and many denominations, I will be providing a resource that encompasses all of the gifts. You can decide how you want to use and implement the following teaching on the gifts into your family and church's life.

A List of Giftings

The key scriptural passages referred to in regard to spiritual gifts are 1 Corinthians 12:7-10,27-28; Ephesians 4:11-12 and Romans 12:6-8.

These passages directly identify certain spiritual abilities as gifts from the Holy Spirit.

A solid scriptural case can also be made for many other spiritual abilities being included in the list of gifts that I and many others present. Some of these would be the spiritual abilities/gifts of celibacy, voluntary poverty, martyrdom, the call of the career missionary, hospitality and craftsmanship. Peter Wagner, who wrote the bestselling *Discover Your Spiritual Gifts,* has added intercession, deliverance and worship leading to his list.[1]

What follows are the Bible's key gifts passages, along with a list of the giftings included in the *Discover Your Kid's Spiritual Gifts* survey:

Now to each one the manifestation of the Spirit is given for the common good. To one there is given through the Spirit the message of *wisdom,* to another the message of *knowledge* by means of the same Spirit, to another *faith* by the same Spirit, to another gifts of healing by that one Spirit, to another miraculous powers, to another prophecy, to another *distinguishing between spirits,* to another speaking in different kinds of tongues, and to still another the interpretation of tongues (1 Cor. 12:7-10, emphasis added).

Now you are the body of Christ, and each one of you is a part of it. And in the church God has appointed first of all *apostles,* second *prophets,* third *teachers,* then *workers of miracles,* also those having gifts of *healing,* those able to help others, those with gifts of *administration,* and those speaking in different kinds of *tongues* (1 Cor. 12:27-28, emphasis added).

It was he [Christ] who gave some to be apostles, some to be prophets, some to be *evangelists,* and some to be *pastors* and *teachers,* to prepare God's people for *works of service,* so that the body of Christ may be built up (Eph. 4:11-12, emphasis added).

We have different gifts, according to the grace given us. If a man's gift is prophesying, let him use it in proportion to his faith. If it is serving, let him serve; if it is teaching, let him teach; if it is *encouraging*, let him encourage; if it is contributing to the needs of others, let him *give* generously; if it is *leadership*, let him govern diligently; if it is showing *mercy*, let him do it cheerfully (Rom. 12:6-8, emphasis added).

Gifts Defined

Administration: The spiritual gift of *administration* is the ability to manage, plan and orchestrate God's purposes upon the earth.

Apostle: The term "apostle" (Greek, *apostolos*) simply means "a sent one." An apostle is a messenger or an ambassador. The idea is that of representation: An apostle is a personal representative for the one(s) who sent him.

Discernment: The spiritual gift of *discernment* allows the believer to rapidly see to the core of an issue and know the truth. This could relate to doctrinal error, a ministry decision, relational and spiritual issues, and so on.

Encouragement: The spiritual gift of *encouragement* is the ability to strengthen another person through words or perhaps physical presence. Encouragers bring comfort and healing to others. They spur them on.

Evangelism: The spiritual gift of *evangelism* is the ability to boldly share the message of salvation in a way that is clear, concise and effective. Evangelists not only share the gospel but also see people make a decision for Christ.

Faith: The spiritual gift of *faith* is a strong belief in the promises and purposes of God. It is the ability to believe in things that are unseen. Hebrews describes faith as not just believing in things unseen, but also of being sure of those things.

Giving: The spiritual gift of *giving* is the ability to give, with a thankful and cheerful heart, from material resources for the purpose of meeting others' needs or accomplishing some purpose.

Healing: The spiritual gift of *healing* is the ability to be used as a conduit for God to deliver supernatural healing and wholeness to another.

Helps: The gift of *helps* is manifested in believers who invest their talents into the life and ministry of others, allowing the one being served to increase in his or her own abilities.

Hospitality: The spiritual gift of *hospitality* equips believers to provide open arms, open houses and a warm welcome for the purpose of encouragement and equipping.

Intercession/Prayer: The gift of *intercession/prayer* is the ability to pray at length and with effectiveness. Intercessors stand in the gap. In the book of Ezekiel, we see God looking for someone who is willing to stand in the gap (see Ezek. 22:30).

Interpretation of Tongues: *Interpretation of tongues* is the ability to understand and communicate in common language the meaning of a tongue given by another member of the Body of Christ.

Knowledge: The spiritual gift of *knowledge* is twofold. It is the ability to grasp deep scriptural truth and it is also a spiritual insight into particular situations.

Leadership: The spiritual gift of *leadership* is the capability to direct God's people into God's plans. Leaders have the capacity to lead beyond themselves.

Mercy: The spiritual gift of *mercy* starts with a heart for the hurting and the outcast. Mercy shows its fruit in taking action to meet the needs of the hurting and despondent.

Miracles: The spiritual gift of *miracles* is the ability to partner with God to see supernatural power influence the natural order of things.

Missions: The spiritual gift of *missions* is the God-given desire and ability to minister effectively in a foreign culture or subculture.

Pastor/Shepherding: The gift of *pastor/shepherding* is the special ability God gives to certain members of the Body of Christ to assume a long-term personal responsibility for the spiritual welfare of others. Pastors nurture, care for and guide people toward progressive spiritual maturity and becoming like Christ.

Prophecy: The spiritual gift of *prophecy* is the ability to understand God's future purposes and plans for His people.

Serving: The spiritual gift of *serving* is the ability to see a need and use whatever resources are at hand to accomplish the task.

Teacher/Teaching: The spiritual gift of *teaching* is the ability to pass on knowledge and concepts to others in a way they can easily grasp and understand.

Tongues: The gift of *tongues* is the ability to speak in a God-given spiritual language that is for the purpose of edifying the Church or being understood by nonbelievers for the purpose of their salvation.

Wisdom: The spiritual gift of *wisdom* allows a believer to make accurate and well-timed decisions. Wisdom incorporates insight into what is true and right with an understanding of how to implement that knowledge into action.

Scriptural Support for Gifts Used in
Discover Your Kid's Spiritual Gifts

1. **Administration:** Exod. 18:13-27; Acts 6:2-4; 1 Cor. 12:28
2. **Apostle:** Acts 14:21-23; 1 Cor. 12:28-29; Eph. 1:1; 4:11
3. **Discernment:** 1 Kings 3:9; Acts 5:3-6; Rom. 12:2; 1 Cor. 2:14; Heb. 5:14; 1 John 4:1
4. **Encouragement:** Acts 4:36; 11:23-24; Rom. 12:8; 1 Thess. 4:18
5. **Evangelism:** Acts 21:8; Eph. 4:11-12; 2 Tim. 4:5
6. **Faith:** Luke 17:5; Rom. 10:17; 1 Cor. 12:9; Phil. 3:9; Heb. 11:1,6
7. **Giving:** Mark 12:43-44; Rom. 12:6,8; 2 Cor. 8:2-3; 9:7
8. **Healing:** Matt. 10:1; Luke 4:40; Acts 3:6-9; 1 Cor. 12:9,30
9. **Helps*:** Acts 6:2-4; 1 Cor. 12:28; 1 Tim. 5:10
10. **Hospitality:** Rom. 12:13; 1 Tim. 3:2; 5:10; Titus 1.8; 1 Pet. 4:9-10
11. **Intercession/Prayer*:** Luke 18:1; John 16:24; Eph. 6:18; 1 Thess. 3:10-13; 5:17; 1 Tim. 2:1-2; 5:5
12. **Interpretation of Tongues:** 1 Cor. 12:10-11,30; 14:5
13. **Knowledge:** John 7:16-17; 17:3; 1 Cor. 12:8; Eph. 3:18-19
14. **Leadership:** Rom. 12:8; Heb. 13:7
15. **Mercy:** Matt. 5:7; Luke 6:36; Rom. 12:8; Titus 3:5
16. **Miracles:** John 20:30-31; Acts 2:22; 19:11; 1 Cor. 12:10
17. **Missions*:** Matt. 28:18-20; Mark 13:10; 16:15; Acts 1:8; 22:21; 1 Cor. 9:19-23
18. **Pastor/Shepherding:** Jer. 23:4; John 10:11; Eph. 4:11-12; 1 Tim. 3:2; Heb. 13:17; 1 Pet. 5:1-4
19. **Prophecy:** Joel 2:28; Rom. 12:6; 1 Cor. 12:10,29; 14:1-3,30-33; Eph. 4:11-12
20. **Serving:** Deut. 10:12; Rom. 12:7; Gal. 6:2; Eph. 3:7; 4:12; 6:7
21. **Teacher/Teaching:** Eph. 4:11-12; 1 Cor. 12:29; Rom. 12:7; Acts 11:25-26; 13:1; 15:35; John 7:16
22. **Tongues:** Acts 2:1-13; 10:44-46; 1 Cor. 12:10-11,28-31; 14:1-5,13-22
23. **Wisdom:** Prov. 3:13; Rom. 11:33; 1 Cor. 12:8; 2 Tim 3:15; Jas. 3:13-18

* Gifts included in the *Discover Your Kid's Spiritual Gifts* spiritual gifts survey but not mentioned in the three key passages of 1 Corinthians 12, Ephesians 4 or Romans 12.

Note: The gifts of Apostle, Tongues and Interpretation of Tongues are not included in the corresponding gifts assessment test. The gift of Apostle is a gifting expressed in adult church leadership. The gifts of tongues and interpretation of tongues, if present, are easily discerned.

Note

1. See C. Peter Wagner, *Your Spiritual Gifts Can Help Your Church Grow* (Ventura, CA: Regal, 2005), pp. 267-274.

Categorizing the Gifts

*Among born again adults, the percentage that say they
have heard of spiritual gifts but do not believe God has given
them one jumped from 4% in 1995 to 21% in 2000.[1]*

THE BARNA GROUP

I have broken up the gifts into five categories.[2] I am sure that you
can find other people who have a different approach and a system
of categorizing, but this should get you started. Please don't just
accept what I or someone else says. Make a personal study of the
gifts from the listed Bible passages and bring your kids along for
the ride. You can never go wrong when embarking on a personal
study of God's Word for yourself.

Spiritual Gifts Category 1—Shepherding: Administration,
Apostle, Teacher/Teaching, Leadership, Pastor/Shepherding

Spiritual Gifts Category 2—Serving: Giving, Helps, Serving, Hospitality

Spiritual Gifts Category 3—Compassion: Encouragement, Healing, Mercy

Spiritual Gifts Category 4—Understanding: Discernment, Tongues and Interpretation of Tongues, Knowledge, Intercession/Prayer, Wisdom, Prophecy

Spiritual Gifts Category 5—Salvation: Evangelism, Faith, Miracles, Tongues (a two-category gift), Missions

Category 1 — Shepherding
Administration, Apostle, Teacher/Teaching, Leadership, Pastor/Shepherding

The shepherding gifts are ones that lend themselves to the care and direction of God's people. The shepherding category contains gifts that are leadership based in nature. With that said, we as Western Christians need to be careful that we do not attach our culture's leadership standards to this gift set or to our children.

As Western parents, when we consider the shepherding gifts, we might easily picture a bold and charismatic figure on a stage and miss the point that some leaders/shepherds lead only one or two individuals at a time. Others lead from behind a desk, administrating events, and cause those open Kingdom doors for others to walk through.

While leadership can mean directing the masses, it is more accurate in the case of spiritual gifts to see the shepherding gifts as directing and caring for God's people according to God's will. Keeping this in mind will help you not to discount a true gift of leadership in your child.

> If your child has one or more of the shepherding gifts, you will notice that he or she has the ability to change the course others follow.

If your child has one or more of the shepherding gifts, you will notice that he or she has the ability to change the course others follow. There are all types of shepherds and many different ways to shepherd. As a parent, what you are trying to discern in your child is if he or she has the ability to lead beyond himself or herself. In other words, does anyone follow your kid's lead?

Category 2: Serving
Giving, Helps, Serving, Hospitality

Children with serving gifts excel at pouring their life out for others. As is true with all of the gifts, each one is given so that the world might have an accurate depiction of Christ through the lives of His followers. As we live out our gifts, we are displaying Christ to the world.

Kids with the serving gifts will be kids who are living out the *kenosis* passage of Philippians 2. *Kenosis* is a Greek word that means "self-emptying," and it was used by Paul to illustrate the kind of life Jesus led:

> If you have any encouragement from being united with Christ, if any comfort from his love, if any fellowship with the Spirit, if any tenderness and compassion, then make my joy complete by being like-minded, having the same love, being one in spirit and purpose. Do nothing out of selfish ambition or vain conceit, but in humility consider others better than yourselves. Each of you should look not only to your own interests, but also to the interests of others. Your attitude should be the same as that of Christ Jesus: Who, being in very nature God, did not consider equality with God something to be grasped, but made himself nothing, taking the very nature of a servant, being made in human likeness. And being found in appearance as a man, he humbled himself and became obedient to death—even death on a cross! Therefore God exalted him to the highest place and gave him the name that is above every name, that at the name of Jesus every knee should bow, in heaven and on earth and under the earth, and every tongue confess that Jesus Christ is Lord, to the glory of God the Father (Phil. 2:1-11).

Unlike the gifts of miracles and tongues, serving is something we are all called to. When you get to heaven, you are not going to be able to tell Jesus that serving was "just not my gift."

Every believer should pray to be a better servant. The only difference with spiritually gifted servant kids is that these acts of serving will come more easily for them and perhaps land with more effectiveness.

Kids who have gifts of serving tend to be less territorial than other kids. The boundary lines between what they claim as theirs, whether time or money, are not very important to them. These are kids who might miss a playground session to go with Mom or Dad to the store and help shop. They often excel at sharing and putting others' needs before their own. While I am not someone who has the supernatural gift of service, I tend to find that the people who do are some of the most attractive believers around. I'm not saying that God sees it that way, but I do.

Category 3: Compassion
Encouragement, Healing, Mercy

If you have ever been in a desperate situation and met a person of compassion, you probably never forgot that person. Mother Teresa is probably the twentieth century's poster child for compassion.

Compassionate people have a way of getting right to the heart of a person and making him or her feel a sense of belonging. I have always experienced compassionate people as having a way of making me feel at ease.

The compassion gifts are endowed with a power to change a person to the core. Compassion can break through tough situations and emotions, bringing hope. In essence, they are a strengthening gift in that they strengthen the interior of a person. This often translates to physical needs as well, because compassionate people are often people of action. Kids with the gift of compassion are often sensitive kids who feel others' pain. They tend to be attentive and seek to alleviate suffering when possible.

A note on healing compassion: You might be wondering why healing is listed in this gift set. This is because healing is often the fruit of compassion. We see this in the life of Christ. More than once in the Gospels, we see Jesus healing others after He took compassion on a group of people. In these instances, it seems as if compassion opened the door for God's healing power to manifest itself.

> When Jesus landed and saw a large crowd, he *had compassion* on them and *healed* their sick (Matt. 14:14, emphasis added).

> Jesus had compassion on them and touched their eyes. Immediately they *received their sight* and followed him (Matt. 20:34, emphasis added).

Compassionate kids are often gentle, but not always. The truest characteristic of a person of compassion is that after his or her heart is touched by another person's need, he or she reacts to meet the need in a way that brings strength, hope and encouragement.

If you study biblical compassion, you will see that it most often ends with a need being met. Ezekiel 16:5 shows this principle in reverse. Here, because no one had compassion, nothing was done:

> No one looked on you with pity or had compassion enough to do any of these things for you. Rather, you were thrown out into the open field, for on the day you were born you were despised.

While I am still unsure about Lucy having the gift of compassion, I had a glimpse into its possible existence the other day. Last week, we headed downtown to Extraordinary Desserts for some sugary decadence. If you ever vacation in San Diego, don't miss this spot. (It is way better than the Zoo or Sea World.)

While downtown, Lucy was confronted with homeless people for the first time. She could not understand why these people did not have houses. Upon seeing many of these people living under tarps, Lucy asked if we could go to the bank and get money to buy houses for them. Her heart had been touched with their need.

What led me to believe that Lucy had a compassion gifting was what happened the next day. She emptied her piggy bank, brought me the contents and told me to buy some houses for these people. This is the heart of compassion. It is empathy plus action.

Isn't that Cute?

If you just read that story and thought, *How cute,* I want you to reconsider that reaction. Too often when we experience our children having real Kingdom-bringing experiences or walking in their giftings, we are tempted to relegate it to the "Oh, how cute!" category.

When we do this, we sometimes miss a moment to truly edify our children in their walk with Christ. As a matter of fact, it actually demeans them and their faith. Moments like these, and the ones you will experience as you awaken to your child's giftings, are holy moments, not just cute stories to tell your friends at your small-group get-together later in the week.

When Lucy made this incredibly selfless and compassionate act, I paused and stopped to edify and encourage my three-year-old. I went on to validate her by telling her that what she had just done was something Jesus would have done. I told her that it was very compassionate. I told her that she might have the spiritual gifts of mercy and giving.

By taking our sons' or daughters' faith and spiritual walk seriously, instances like this when God is touching your child's heart can go from a momentary event to becoming another building block in affirming who Christ has made your child to be. You can do this every time you see your child walking according to the Spirit, each time solidifying them in their faith and fashioning its sustainability.

Being a parent who regularly affirms Christ's workings in your children will help them build a sense of Kingdom belonging. It will let them know who they are.

Category 4: Understanding

Discernment, Interpretation of Tongues, Knowledge, Intercession/Prayer, Wisdom, Prophecy, Tongues (also in gifts of salvation)

If you are not part of the 50 percent of Protestant believers who espouse the more charismatic gifts of understanding,[3] this gift set might seem a reach for you. I would still encourage you to read through them to see what the other camp believes.

The gifts of understanding are all about perspective. They are about God's perspective spoken to a broken humanity. When a child asserts a gift of understanding or spiritual insight, he or she is conveying a heavenly perspective to a given situation. The gifts of understanding exist for the purpose of communication. God uses these gifts to communicate with His people. These gifts often explain how God wants to implement scriptural truth into real-life situations. For instance, the Bible tells us to love, but a word of knowledge might tell us whom God wants us to love and the manner in which to do it.

So how does God speak to us? All Christians believe that God speaks to His people. The way in which He speaks is what is up for conjecture. God speaks in many ways; He is, after all, infinite and not limited in any way. The key to rightly using the gifts of understanding is to make sure that everything discerned stands up against Scripture. In this way, Scripture maintains its rightful place as the central source of revelation. If a word of prophecy or a tongue is given, it needs to agree with the whole teaching of God's final Word. The same is true with worship songs or a good friend's advice. God uses both to communicate with us, but each must stand the test of Scripture in order to be accepted.

Many people have limited this category of gifting. This viewpoint, called "cessationism," holds that gifts like tongues and miracles were for the launching of the Church as described in the book of Acts, but their season is now over and God has removed these gifts from the Church's spiritual palate. I'm not writing to prove or argue these points. Rather, I simply want to explain how to identify and engage your children in their personal giftings according to your system of belief. Once again, if your personal or denominational stance conflicts with this understanding, just move on. The key is to get your child into the ministry you see corresponding to their gifts.

With that said, a child who displays the gifts of understanding will say things beyond his or her years. This child will have insights that speak God's truth. It might be in regard to a certain situation your family is going through, or a scriptural perspective revealing deep truth. Some kids might have dreams or visions or be aware of spiritual attack.

I regularly hear parents tell stories of these types of spiritual insights and understandings. Often, these parents are taken aback by what their children have said. They seem to know that God was part of that insight, but they just don't know what to do about it. As we move forward, I will help you with this. My goal is to give you tools to build a platform for your child to grow in these and other giftings, always keeping an eye on the central purpose of the gifts, which is to demonstrate God's love to others:

> If I have the gift of prophecy and can fathom all mysteries and all knowledge, and if I have a faith that can move mountains, but have not love, I am nothing (1 Cor. 13:2).

Category 5: Salvation
Evangelism, Faith, Miracles, Tongues, Missions

Salvific gifts are those gifts that lead people to Christ. Granted, all of the gifts can potentially lead people to knowledge of Jesus, but these gifts are specifically geared to change a person's eternal position. People with the gifts of salvation are soul winners. They have a concern for the lost and are bold in the sharing of that gift.

I have met many kids who are playground evangelists. These are kids who want to talk about Jesus to the point that it sometimes makes their parents uncomfortable. (Does this describe your kid?) These children are quick to invite a friend to church. They often come home and share about conversations they have had with unsaved friends. They are hungry for the gospel.

Oddly, I have seen more small children walk in evangelistic gifts than teenagers (I was a youth pastor to teens for more than a decade). I think one of the reasons for this is that many parents don't know how to set this gift aflame when it presents itself in younger children. The danger I have found is that our gifts have a tendency to flourish or wither in accordance with our stewarding of them.

I would argue that if a child has a gifting in any area, that gift should be growing exponentially as the child develops. Kids, like adults, should mature in their faith. This happens when they are being nurtured in their gifts and their walk with Christ. Just filling our kids with knowledge of Jesus and the Scriptures does not accomplish this. Even demons are accredited with this ability! Instead, we need to make sure that our sons and daughters are getting their spiritual hands dirty by expressing their gifts within a hurting and broken world.

> You believe that there is one God. Good! Even the demons believe that—and shudder (Jas. 2:19).

Developing the Gifts of Evangelism

How many children do you know who can lead a friend to Jesus using an understanding of the Scriptures? Is it too much to expect our kids to know a handful of verses they could use to more accurately share the gospel with friends? We expect at least this much competency in so many other academic areas of their life. Should we not also equip them in a knowledge of Scripture that goes beyond the ability to quote John 3:16?

I am of the thinking that if my eight-year-old is expected to learn her times tables and memorize a thousand or so words for spelling tests this year, she can also learn the core Bible verses that apply to salvation. The problem I have faced is that I am often more committed to Lily's weekly spelling test than I am to her knowledge of God's Word.

It's not a surprise that many kids have such a weak understanding of the Scriptures. I have found that most adult believers cannot even systematically take you through six to eight verses that accurately present the gospel. While it is a hard statement, I would argue that if you cannot present a simple verse-by-verse gospel presentation, you are dangerously close to being scripturally illiterate. Is not the gospel the essence of our faith? Is it too much to ask for Christians to be able to present the gospel according to God's Word?

> While it is a hard statement, I would argue that if you cannot present a simple verse-by-verse gospel presentation, you are dangerously close to being scripturally illiterate.

What about you as a parent? Can you jot down six to eight verses right now off the top of your head that you could use to clearly relate the core of the gospel to a friend or co-worker? If not, you now have a great discipleship opportunity in front of you. You won't have to search too far on the Internet to find all you need to get started winning souls to Christ with your kids.

As We Go Forward

In the next chapter, we are going to begin to dissect each of the spiritual gifts. Before we get to that, I want you to think about your child in regard to the larger gift categories.

Pull away from all distractions and interruptions for half an hour or so and begin to think about your child in light of the five spiritual aptitudes you have just read about: shepherding, serving, compassion, understanding and salvation.

Use your journal or iPad to jot down anything that came to mind as you read this chapter. Perhaps you recall something that happened this week that resonated with what you were reading. Perhaps what resonated with your soul was something God gave you as insight into your child's spiritual gifting.

Maybe someone else has given you a word of insight or Scripture about your child that seemed to sit well with your soul. Write it down. There is no harm in journaling insights to be prayed over and tested in the future.

At this point, the object is not that you identify a pinpoint description of your kid's spiritual gifts, but rather that you begin to seek the LORD for insight and truth related to this subject.

Later, when we look at the biblical examples of the lives of Hannah, Isaac, Rebekah and Mary the mother of Christ, we will see that God often gives discernment to parents long before they ever meet their kids. This is just one of the ways that God equips us to raise our children to be men and women of God. He directs us as parents in the way that our children should go so that we can in turn guide them in that path:

> Train a child in the way he should go, and when he is old he will not turn from it (Prov. 22:6).

While it is not a new teaching, many believe that this verse not only refers to training up a child in the ways, laws and grace of our God, but also training them in their personal callings. I would affirm this understanding.

A Prayer for Understanding

Dear God, I pray that You would begin to guide me as I seek You for my child. What do You want me to know about [insert name]? What giftings have You graced [name] with? Would You begin to show me his [her] unique position in the Kingdom so that I might be able to lead him into this purpose? Finally, would You equip me with wisdom, knowledge, discernment and understanding so that I might be aware of what You are doing in his life? Please speak to me in this time!

For years, I have used Psalm 139 to pray for people. In the text below, I have created a prayer that you can use to pray for insight into your child's life. I have changed many of the first-person pronouns to second-person pronouns to reflect your desire to hear from God for your child. For ease of reading, I have used only one

gender pronoun (see the words in bold); use the appropriate gender pronoun for your child. Some pronouns have been left intact
to reflect you as the seeking intercessor. Verses 19-22 are removed
from the prayer, but if you feel the need to slay some of the wicked,
feel free to add them back in!

O Lord, you have searched my child and you know **him**.

You know when **he** sits and when **he** rises; you perceive **his**
thoughts from afar.

You discern **his** going out and **his** lying down; you are familiar with all of **his** ways.

Before a word is on **his** tongue you know it completely, O
Lord.

You hem **him** in—behind and before; you have laid your
hand upon **him**.

Such knowledge is too wonderful for me, too lofty for me
to attain.

Where can **he** go from your Spirit? Where can **he** flee from
your presence?

If **he** goes up to the heavens, you are there; if **he** makes **his**
bed in the depths, you are there.

If **he** rises on the wings of the dawn, if he settles on the far
side of the sea,

even there your hand will guide **his**, your right hand will
hold **his** fast.

If **he** says, "Surely the darkness will hide **me** and the light
become night around **me**,"

even the darkness will not be dark to you; the night will
shine like the day, for darkness is as light to you.

For you created **his** inmost being; you knit **him** together
in **his** mother's womb.

I praise you because **he is** fearfully and wonderfully made;
your works are wonderful, I know that full well.

His frame was not hidden from you when **he was** made
in the secret place. When **he** was woven together in the
depths of the earth,

your eyes saw **his** unformed body. All the days ordained
for **him** were written in your book before one of them
came to be.

How precious to me are your thoughts, O God! How vast
is the sum of them! Were I to count them, they would
outnumber the grains of sand. When I awake, I am still
with you. . . .

Search me, O God, and know my heart; test me and know
my anxious thoughts [about my children's future].

See if there is any offensive way in me, and lead me in the
way everlasting.

This is also a great bedtime prayer to pray over your children.
It is just so affirming. Lay your hands on your child and add his or
her name into the text. May God greatly increase your insight into
your children's spiritual gifting for the advancement of God's
kingdom!

Notes

1. "Awareness of Spiritual Gifts Is Changing," The Barna Group, February 5, 2001. http://www.barna.org/barna-update/article/5-barna-update/32-awareness-of-spiri tual-gifts-is-changing.

2. "Pentecostal Resource Page," Pew Forum on Religion and Public Life, October 5, 2006. http://pewforum.org/Christian/Evangelical-Protestant-Churches/Pentecostal-Resource-Page.aspx.

3. See Rusty Freeman's spiritual gifts survey, which can be found at http://www.reach-ingyouth.org/f/Spiritual_Gifts_Inventory_ Revised.pdf.

PART TWO

Recognizing Spiritual Gifts in Kids

This is how I started a big part of my life with God. One day when I was playing with my friend Halle, I said something that got her really upset. I probably shouldn't have said it. We got into a big fight that went on and on. Then one day, she came up to me and said that she didn't believe in God. She said that because she knew that I loved God more than anything. Even though the fight wasn't about God, she just wanted me to get upset.

Day after day she kept saying it, until she believed what she said. So for a few weeks I taught her about God. I told her that God had power over everything, even the devil. I talked to my mom and dad about it. I used the Bible and told Halle that God loved and cared for everyone, even the people that don't know who God is. When I told her everything about God and heaven, she finally believed in God again! That is how I started my big part of life with God!

Jaden, Age 9
Playground Evangelist

Shepherds and Flocks

The Shepherding Gifts

But as for me, I have not hurried away from being a shepherd *after You.*
(JEREMIAH 17:16, EMPHASIS ADDED)

Spiritual Gifts Category 1: Shepherding
Administration, Apostle, Teacher/Teaching, Leadership, Pastor/Shepherding

Outside of Jesus, David was arguably the most gifted kid we see in the pages of Scripture. Actually, there is a lot more known scripturally about David's childhood than that of Jesus. When we look at David as a boy we see a very unique and powerful gift mix. David was a pastor, leader, prophet, teacher, man of wisdom, discerner of spirits . . . the list goes on. All of these gifts were understood by David and employed when he was a child. David never would have been the adult king he became if this had not been the case.

While it is true that David was born to be king, we must remember that God used David's time as a shepherd as training ground for that calling. While David was incredibly gifted in many ways, he was always a shepherd at heart.

Recently, I heard a pastor give a message about the difference between shepherds and ranchers in light of church leadership. He said that shepherds are seen as giving their congregations quality care. But the downside of being a shepherd is their inability to lead congregations beyond a certain number of people.

Ranchers, on the other hand, are portrayed as leaders who have the ability to lead large groups. Ranchers delegate the individual care of people to ranch hands so that they can focus on the larger vision task at hand.

David was a pastor, leader, prophet, teacher, man of wisdom, discerner of spirits . . . the list goes on. All of these gifts were understood by David and employed when he was a child. David never would have been the adult king he became if this had not been the case.

I'm not sure that King David would fit solely into either of these categories. David had the ability to govern the nation of God, but who would argue that he was not truly a shepherd at his core?

As we unpack the shepherding gifts, note that each of the gifts loses power when not employed with the care of individual people as their purpose. As you discover and lead your child into his or her potential shepherding gift, make sure that you drive this point home. Loving God's people is always the point of any shepherding gift. When we lose sight of that, we can easily make our ministry about ourselves. Then the kingdom we are building is not God's, but our own.

(Note: Your child can have a strong pastoral gift and not be called into full-time pastoral ministry. This can also be true with other gifts, like the missionary gifting. Missionaries don't have to be called to Africa to express their calling. Some missionaries are called to subcultures within their own culture and geographical location.)

Administration

Administration is the ability to manage, plan and orchestrate God's purposes upon the earth.

Administrators are those individuals who can take a leader's vision or personal prompting from God and make it happen through organization. If a leader is not present, administrators are often willing to fulfill that role, but they are not as comfortable in it. Administrators are systems creators. Kids who have the spiritual gift of administration show an attention to detail and take joy in helping others put plans into place.

Spotting the gift of administration in your child is one of the easiest of the spiritual gifts to recognize. Like kids who are talented in the area of sports, kids with administrational giftings are pretty hard to miss.

Imagine taking 20 kids and dropping them into a makeshift game of soccer or dodge ball. In less than five minutes, you will be able to recognize athletically gifted kids.

The same can be said for most of the gifts, but especially the gift of administration. This is why the best way to test gifts is on the field of play for that prospective gifting. It is usually pretty easy to see which kids excel in each of the gifts.

For really young kids, you might want to observe how they organize their play things. Does your child like organized systems or does he or she let everything fly to the wind? For older kids, the way in which they organize their schoolwork might easily point to their ability to organize and administrate.

One great way to test this gift is to ask your kid to plan something. Ask your child to organize his or her toys or some other household project according to a system of his or her choosing. See if your child dives into this task and creates an organized system. If you have an older child, let him or her have a hand in administering an upcoming birthday or holiday event. Simple exercises and challenges like this can help you identify if your kid has the ability to manage and administrate for the kingdom of God.

Your kid might have the gift of administration if you observe the following patterns:

- Likes detail. When you share details, he or she tends to focus in on those.
- Tends to keep his or her things organized. Small kids might keep their toys categorized according to different patterns. I have a friend whose kid keeps all the ponies

in one corner, lions in another, and so on. Be aware of how your kids organize their things.
- Offers a solution for doing something more effectively and efficiently.
- Makes lists.
- Tends to be responsible with the things he or she is delegated, such as chores.
- Often desires to work under instruction as opposed to leading directly. Usually asks for more details, hoping to understand the task better.
- Has a visionary's ability to see the end result of a project for possible pitfalls.
- Has the ability to be decisive.

Apostle

The term "apostle" (Greek, *apostolos*) simply means "a sent one." An apostle is a messenger, an ambassador. The idea is that of representation: An apostle is a personal representative for the one(s) who sent him.

There is a lot of debate surrounding this particular gifting. The reason for this debate centers on the authority that comes with being considered an apostle. The well-trodden argument for only accepting the ancient understanding of apostleship is that the term "apostle" referred only to those who had actually spent personal time with Jesus. This is what we see espoused in the following selected portions of an article from biblicalstudies.com:

Like the gift of Pastor-Teacher, one was an apostle not only by calling or gifting but also by meeting certain qualifications. As already noted in the previous chapter, an apostle must have been one who could personally testify to the risen Christ. This was Paul's argument in 1 Corinthians 9:1, which established his own apostleship: "Have I not seen Jesus our Lord?" This was also one of the requirements stipulated by the eleven for the replacement of Judas (Acts 1:21-22). The credentials of Christ's apostles also included the ability to perform miracles. Jesus Himself gave this power to the

twelve when He commissioned them (Matthew 10:1). Again
in defending his apostleship to the Corinthians Paul mentioned this as something which identified him as a true
apostle: "Truly the signs of an apostle were wrought among
you in all patience, in signs, and wonders, and mighty deeds"
(2 Cor. 12:12, *KJV*). The apostles were miracle workers who
could bear personal witness to the risen Lord.[1]

Others, like C. Peter Wagner, believe that the gift of apostleship
is fully alive and well in this era. The premise is that God still sends
people into the world with specific messages and callings to create
or accomplish a special work of God.

In Wagner's book *Apostles of the City,* he attempts to describe what
the local role of these apostles might be. He defines Apostles to the
City as those "whom the Holy Spirit gives an anointing for extraordinary authority in spiritual matters over the other Christian leaders
in the same city." While not excluding others, Wagner hypothesizes
that the most extensive pool for identifying apostles of the city is
among the mega churches.[2]

While I do think that it is possible that God has anointed some
believers with this modern understanding of the gift of apostleship,
I get hung up on the authority aspect that some churches highlight.

We need to be careful when a human being is seen as having a direct line to God that is not available to the rest of us. True, God sends
certain people with certain messages at certain times, but I believe
that if the apostleship gifting is available today it would have to be
under the authority of the community of believers. What an apostle
brings to the table has to ring true in the ears of those who surround
the apostle. The message must also hold to Scripture. Without these
checks and balances in place, there is a tendency to begin following
a man or a woman, rather than God.

Because I know many of our charismatic and Pentecostal broth-
ers and sisters honor this gift, I have added it to my list of giftings.

(Note: I have not added Apostle to the actual spiritual gifts test
I have created. It proved difficult to test for in children and seemed
to give false positive readings for the leadership gift. I would also

state that this gift is one that deals directly with leading leaders within the adult church setting. Thus, you would not truly be able to discern this until a person begins to express a direct call to vocational ministry.)

Your child might have the gift of Apostle if you notice the following patterns:

- Has the ability to share God's message of hope and direction to others
- Often shares things he/she feels that God has laid on his or her heart
- Seems to walk in a God-given authority
- Is clear about God's purposes for the Church and his or her position in it
- Holds a place of respect among his or her believing peers
- Has a bigger vision for the works of God than most kids (school, city, country, world)

Teaching

The spiritual gift of *teaching* is the ability to pass on knowledge and concepts to others in a way they can easily grasp and understand.

Where would we be without teachers? Einstein, when speaking about this crucial ability, said, "If you can't explain it to a six-year-old, you don't understand it yourself."[3] That is what teachers do. Teachers take complex things and make them simply understandable.

When Lily was in first grade, she had a "Big Buddy" named Sophia. Sophia was part of an interscholastic program where older kids came into the classes of younger students as tutors.

Lily loved Sophia. And not only did Sophia love Lily back, but she was also a fantastic tutor. When I found out later that Sophia was a believer, it occurred to me that she most likely had the gift of teaching.

My thought is this: If the public school system can see an aptitude in a child and create a program for her to grow in this gifting, why can't we do the same as the Church? As believers we need not let the standards of the world rank higher than our own.

When Lily became a third-grader, she also became a big buddy. It is something she loves. After watching her patience and aptitude in teaching her little sister things, I decided to provide a platform to test this gift further.

Test everything. Hold on to the good (1 Thess. 5:21).

About a month ago, I asked Lily if she would like to teach the preschool Sunday School lesson. This class has about 30 kids in it. I asked our children's pastor, Jason, about it. He was excited about the idea of allowing Lily to test her gifts, so we set it up.

This is just one example of how you can begin to test the gifts you see in your kids. There are plenty of ways to do this, but the key is to test something your child wants to do. Yes, there is a balance, but you don't want to push your kids into ministry. Let me repeat that. Do not push your kids into ministry. Rather, challenge them into their calling! Usually, if there is a gifting present, it will be something your child naturally wants to do. Enthusiasm for something can be a good barometer to potential gifting.

By the way, Lily did great. She was super-nervous, but with a little help from me, the message got across. Lots of kids asked questions, and Lily felt like the experiment was a success. I'll be setting up another opportunity soon. You can do this type of experiment with any gifting you see within your kids. Perhaps it will become their ministry.

A kid with the gift of teaching might display the following pattern:

- Tends to use stories, word pictures or analogies when describing things.
- When doing a task for someone, he or she will often explain the task as opposed to doing it without an explanation.
- Desires deeper understanding.
- Can be passionate about correcting errors.
- Communicates verbally or through the written word with great clarity.
- Others respond and learn from what he or she has taught.
- Loves to see others grasp what he or she is trying to communicate.

- Is excited about Scripture and its nuances.
- Has insights into Scripture that others do not see. You might be surprised when he or she discovers something you did not realize when discussing God's Word with him/her.

Leadership

The spiritual gift of *leadership* is the capability to direct God's people into God's plans. Leaders have the capacity to lead beyond themselves.

Leadership is one of the most valued characteristics in Western culture. From an early age, many of us are told that we should be leaders and not followers. This is an odd statement since it is a physical impossibility. Society and the church could never function like this. We can't all be leaders.

One thing you never hear parents implore their kids to be is a great follower. "Hey, Johnny, go out and be the best follower you can be!" But this is what some parents should be telling their kids. Instead, many parents implore their kids to be great leaders when they might actually be called to be world-changing followers, like David's Mighty Men (see 2 Sam. 23).

Instead of telling all of our kids to be great leaders, we should teach them discernment on how to identify leaders they might want to follow. There is no shame in being a follower. Most of the people in the world are followers. The key is teaching our kids discernment of what and who to follow.

With that said, some kids are spiritually gifted leaders. Your child might be one of them. Sure, we will all experience a time in life when God challenges us to lead, but having the spiritual gift of leadership is a whole different gig.

Leaders have the ability to grasp the way of God, His plans and purposes, and communicate them in a way that causes others to follow. Leaders are course charters and inspire course correction in others.

Leaders come in all shapes and sizes. Jack Dorsey, the founder and CEO of Twitter, is not your typical leader, but I am sure he has more "followers" than most leaders ever will.[4] Dorsey is quiet, reserved and brilliant. He is not a traditional type of charismatic figure leading the masses. Instead, Dorsey has led the world through technology, one tweet at a time.

I had the opportunity to hear Jack Dorsey interviewed at Catalyst West Coast. Catalyst is a conference for Christian leaders. Dorsey noted that his greatest strength as a leader was the ability to understand when culture and technology were intersecting. Dorsey was able to create a platform the masses could use to access that technology. No matter what you think about "Tweeting," you cannot argue with Jack Dorsey's ability to lead people in a direction. Twitter is currently on pace to reach 200 million users before the year 2012.[5]

If you want to see if your kid has the gift of leadership, take him or her and five friends to Disneyland or some other theme park. The night before you go, give them a map of the park and tell them to decide the game plan for the following day. Provide some popcorn and drinks and sit back and watch the fun. If your kid or another in the group begins to take the reins, he or she might have the gift of leadership. You might also see an administrator emerge in this process. That kid will be the one who is inspired by the leader's plan and organizes all of the vision into workable systems. If the leader and the administrator start fighting and biting each other, you might want to step in!

If your child has the spiritual gift of leadership, you might recognize it in the following ways:

- They tend to be initiators.
- They are creative in their vision.
- They are problem solvers. When they come to a roadblock of some kind, they seek ways to innovate around that obstacle.
- They tend to be assertive.
- They are visionaries. They can see and communicate what others don't see.
- When playing with friends, they will come up with new ideas for the group and seek buy-in from others.
- They often think they are right.
- On a family trip to the zoo, they would be the ones who are most verbal about what they want everyone to go and see.
- Leaders will often talk about the future.

Pastor/Shepherding

The gift of *pastor/shepherding* is the special ability God gives to certain members of the Body of Christ to assume a long-term personal responsibility for the spiritual welfare of others. Pastors nurture, care for and guide people toward progressive spiritual maturity and becoming like Christ.[6]

While the dynamic leadership of some people has inspired many of us, it is often the pastors in our lives who touch us most deeply. If you have been in the church for any length of time, you know what I am talking about. Pastors are shepherds who are willing to leave the 99 in order to save the 1. Pastors are the ones who seem to care the most. If you need someone to come to your aid in a desperate time, it is the pastor you will call. Pastors see the Great Commission (see Matt. 28:19-20) starting with the person standing in front of them rather than an entire continent.

Pastors/shepherds are leaders in that they have a flock. If your child has a shepherding gift, he or she will be surrounded by or have influence in the lives of others. Others will look to your child for strength, wisdom and encouragement. Like a shepherd, your kids will tend to their flock. They will care about their needs. Shepherds look for opportunities to meet needs.

If your kid has a pastoral gift, it will manifest itself differently than a gift of leadership. Yes, pastors are leaders, but they lead in a way that touches people in deeply personal ways. Leaders, on the other hand, are often flying at 35,000 feet, and the individual needs of people might get marginalized to fulfill the bigger vision. True pastors, however, are not content to lead in this way.

Even though I have been called by the title of "pastor" for close to two decades, I only recently believed that I received the corresponding gifting. For years I have been an effective leader/teacher, but I was aware that something was lacking in my ability to pastor people. My ministry looked successful on the outside, but it was lacking the personal care I valued in other ministries of which I had been a part. To remedy this, I began to pray that God would help me to love people more. This simple prayer has changed my life as much as any other prayer I have ever prayed.

In the last two years, God has done a tremendous work in my heart and ministry. People have begun to encourage me in my pastoral effectiveness. The only reason I can see for this is that God, through His grace, has given me a new post-conversion gifting. God has truly given me a pastor's heart. I'm no longer content with people falling through the cracks for the sake of a bigger, brighter ministry. I am loving ministry more than I ever have!

If there is a particular gift that you desire, ask God for it. Paul tells us in 1 Corinthians 12:31 to "eagerly desire the greater gifts"; he implores us to desire giftings that we don't yet have. James encourages us to ask for wisdom, which is also a gifting (see Jas. 1:5). God is the giver of gifts and can give you a new gift at any time! Pray the same types of prayers for your kids.

The pastor/shepherd gift does not mean that your child will be in vocational ministry. God showed me a long time ago that He has commissioned shepherds in every area of society. God has released His shepherds throughout the world, and many of them will never wear the title of pastor.

One of the ways the LORD showed me this is through the people who clean the world's churches. Here's what I mean. Some of the most amazing pastors I have ever met have been those who hold a broom and not a Bible in their hands. Over a period of 10 years, and on many continents, I have met these amazing pastors who were content to let the guise of being a doorkeeper in the house of the Lord mask what they were truly passionate about—people.

Some of the most impactful moments in my life have been with these pastors. I have found that they often care for and are in better tune with the heart of a congregation than many staff pastors. These pastors intercede as they mop. They pray for the sick and offer coffee and water to those who come in off the street looking for the church's support.

Your child might never pastor beyond his or her playground, sports team or place of work, but in the Kingdom economy, you can bet that God has a special anointing for the flock your child keeps watch over. May God bless the blacktop and schoolyard shepherds in our midst!

Your kid might have the spiritual gift of pastor/shepherd if you notice a pattern of behavior consisting of the following:

- Sticks up for others.
- Is a good listener.
- Feels others' pain and suffering.
- Tends to say things to let others know that he or she cares. You might find kids with a strong pastoral gift often asking questions about how others are doing or how their day went.
- Helps others respond to life.
- Responds to meet needs.
- Doesn't like to leave anyone behind. We experience this with Lucy. She is always concerned that everyone is coming on a trip.
- Might stop homework or a fun project to help care for another person. This could also be the gift of serving, but the pastoral gifting will go beyond just helping out; there will be a level of care or concern for the individual.
- Is nurturing and caring. While it seems odd, I think one of the best ways to see this gift displayed is with pets. How do your kids respond to your pets? Hey, they don't call them shepherds for nothing. If your kids are gentle and caring with pets, I would lay denari on it that they are shepherds.

Notes

1. "Apostleship," Word of Life Baptist Church. http://www.biblicalstudies.com/bstudy/spiritualgifts/ch14.htm.
2. C. Peter Wagner, *Apostles of the City* (Colorado Springs, CO: Wagner Publications, 2000).
3. See http://www.goodreads.com/quotes/show/19421.
4. Twitter uses the term "followers" to describe those who subscribe to a person's "tweets."
5. Mark Raby, "Twitter on Pace to Reach . . . 200 Million Users by 2011," TG Daily. http://www.tgdaily.com/software-brief/52284-twitter-on-pace-to-reach200-million-users-by-2011.
6. "What Is the Gift of Shepherding?" Cyberspace Ministry. http://www.cyberspace ministry.org/Services/Gifts/eng/eng-shep.html.

6

The Hands and Feet of the Church

The Serving Gifts

The best kings often start out as servants.
The best servants never strive to be kings.

Spiritual Gifts Category 2: Serving
Giving, Helping, Serving, Hospitality

David was a king and man after God's own heart. He assumed the throne the hard way, through patience and a healthy respect for God's anointed. David never took the kingdom; it was given to him.

David's journey to the throne room began as a servant, first carrying supplies to King Saul's troops at the front lines of battle and then as personal worship steward to the king. David displayed the gift of serving as a boy. Because of this, later in life, David kept a heart for the lowly and downcast. David understood the ways and doubts of the serf. It was this understanding that created the king he would become. Later, Jesus followed this pattern in His earthly ministry. The best kings often start out as servants. The best servants never strive to be kings.

> Just as the Son of Man did not come to be served, *but to serve,* and to give his life as a ransom for many (Matt. 20:28, emphasis added).

Hands and Feet for the Sake of Love

The paradox of the servant is that the more they serve and become the least, the greater their value to the Kingdom. Serving is the only investment where you give everything away and end up with all the riches of eternity. In Luke 22, Jesus pointed to servants having a special place in the kingdom of God:

> But you are not to be like that. Instead, the greatest among you should be like the youngest, and the one who rules like the one who serves. For who is greater, the one who is at the table or the one who serves? Is it not the one who is at the table? But I am among you as one who serves (Luke 22:26-27).

When a servant's gifts are under the direction of the Holy Spirit, his or her actions will not serve self, but rather release the love of God to a broken world. We see this in Jesus' washing of the disciples' feet.

In the beginning of this passage (see John 13), Christ forecasts His coming death. On the cross, Jesus would soon show the world the full extent of His love. His act of washing His disciples' feet was meant to point to this larger act of service and love.

Here we see that the point of all spiritual gifts is love. When Jesus served in the washing of feet, it was done for love's sake. Gifts of service cause believers to be greatest in the kingdom of heaven because these acts of self-sacrifice mimic the greatest act of service and love ever done. Jesus intertwined service and love when He died on the cross for our sins. This is why servants hold such high esteem in the kingdom of heaven. Servants most closely represent Jesus' divine purpose and nature.

> It was just before the Passover Feast. Jesus knew that the time had come for him to leave this world and go to the Father. Having loved his own who were in the world, he now showed them the full extent of his love (John 13:1).

Jesus tagged His act of service to the disciples by promising them blessings if they followed His example.

> Now that I, your Lord and Teacher, have washed your feet, you also should wash one another's feet. I have set you an example that you should do as I have done for you. I tell you the truth, no servant is greater than his master, nor is a messenger greater than the one who sent him. Now that you know these things, you will be blessed if you do them (John 13:14-17).

If you want to live under the promise of blessing, then serve. With that said, let's take a look at the primary serving gifts.

Giving

The spiritual gift of *giving* is the ability to give, with a thankful and cheerful heart, from material resources for the purpose of meeting others' needs or accomplishing some purpose.

When the spiritual gift of giving is under submission to the Holy Spirit, it translates into a selfless life that claims little as its own. This is different from dysfunctional people pleasing. The expression of the true spiritual gift of giving gives out of an understanding that everything belongs to God. Because of this, the boundary lines of what kids with the gift of giving claim as their own get blurred. These spiritually gifted kids are more willing to go without, and they share without expecting a return. These kids love seeing others' dreams fulfilled by self-sacrificing love. They are a gift from God to this world, relieving suffering through contribution. They find their joy in pouring out their resources for God's glory.

Our friends Ricky and Destiny have worked to indentify spiritual gifts in their kids. Here is an email about their daughter Ruby's gift of giving:

> Hey Adam,
> When Ruby was two, she would insist on sending her friends home with one of her toys. The mothers were

always dismayed, thinking it was a childish phase and that she would change her mind later. She never did, and would be very hurt if her friends didn't take the toys. She ran out of Barbies and Ponies very quickly! Now she sends them home with shoes, hair ribbons, Polly Pockets, drawings, stickers, whatever she can give, as long as nobody ever leaves our home empty-handed. She also makes cards or packages up cookies and delivers them in her wagon to all the neighbors.

Pretty cool stuff!

Your kid might have the spiritual gift of giving if you notice the following:

- He/she shares.
- Is not overly protective of his/her things.
- Notices and mentions opportunities to give.
- Encourages others to give their things away.
- Doesn't need to have the best in regard to things or possessions.
- Is often content with what he/she has.
- If you take this child to a store to buy something, he/she might mention another person you could get something for as well.
- Is less self-focused than most kids.
- Gives his or her money away.
- May tend to live simply.

Helps

The gift of *helps* is manifested in believers who invest their talents into the life and ministry of others, often allowing the one being served to increase in his or her own abilities.

The gift of helps differs from the gift of service in that its primary aim is to come alongside a person by enabling him or her to accomplish some task or goal. Helpers love to be in the trenches with whomever they are helping. These kids might also have a corresponding gift of teaching. This is because they often want to equip another person while coming alongside to help.

In contrast, children with the gift of service might be more focused on getting the task done for the sake of the cause rather than for the purpose of partnering with the persons they are helping. Helpers, however, love to do things together. They have a passion to see others equipped and aided through their helping. Helpers want to see others grow in their abilities and effectiveness.

Kids with the gift of helps will come alongside other kids to help them accomplish a task. This could be anything from pushing something up a hill to helping a sibling clean his or her room. If your kid reaches out when others need help, he or she may very likely have the gift of helps.

Remember Ruby, from the gift of giving? Seems that this six-year-old also has the gift of helps. Read more from Rick and Destiny's email:

> Ruby always wants to help, asking me every night if she can help me make dinner. If I give her a task, she's so happy to help but doesn't want lavish praise, as it makes her uncomfortable.

Your kid might also have the gift of helps if you notice the following pattern:

- Likes to do things in partnership.
- Offers to help with things like bringing in the groceries and yard work.
- Foresees and mentions possible ways to aid a person when he or she hears of a future need.
- When he or she sees a stranger in need, suggests ways to help the person directly and immediately.
- There is a noticeable change in his or her demeanor when in the midst of helping others. He or she seems to come alive.
- When he or she offers to help, the project or cause he or she is involved with is made noticeably better because of his or her contribution.

Serving/Service

The spiritual gift of *serving* is the ability to see a need and use whatever resources are at hand to accomplish the task.

Believing kids with the spiritual gift of service will do just about anything for the sake of others. Unlike helps, there is not the emphasis on coming alongside someone to see them sharpened. Servants just want to see what needs to get done completed.

I have noticed that truly gifted servants are willing to step out of their comfort zone and try something that other believers might hesitate to do. If there is no one else for the job, the person with the gift of service will offer to step up and see the job accomplished, no matter how dirty, because filling a need is the very nature of this gift. The particular task does not matter.

Paul, in Roman's 12:7, uses the Greek word *diakonia*. This word means to serve or minister to others.[1] It is the quality of being able to dispense to others what is needed in the moment.

If your kids are servants, they will be dedicated to the task at hand. They don't mind working under someone's supervision, and they never feel less for doing so.

Servants are great at volunteering. They won't put a value on the size of the task, but on the completion of it. Servants rarely leave a job half done. These are committed kids who, when serving in the Spirit, as opposed to the flesh, won't beg you for approval or kudos when the job is done.

Your kid might have the gift of service if you notice the following pattern:

- Offers to serve even when the task is something he or she does not naturally excel at.
- Picks up after others.
- Volunteers readily.
- Cleans up when not asked.
- Puts his or her dishes away after dinner.
- When starting a job, he or she tends to finish it.
- Teachers mention that he or she is helpful in class.
- Is attentive to people in need.

- Offers suggestions of what could be done for a person in need.
- Is selfless.
- Doesn't mind working under direction.
- When working to complete a task, he or she is focused and cheerful.

Hospitality

The spiritual gift of *hospitality* equips believers to provide open arms, open houses and a warm welcome for the purpose of encouragement and equipping.

Yesterday, we had a meeting for small-groups training and served dessert. Tanya is our small-groups director and coordinator. I watched Tanya get all of the preparations ready for the event. As people began to enter the room, she continued to make sure everything was done with quality and excellence. Next, Tanya went over her notes to prepare for her presentation.

What gifts would you say Tanya has? If you said hospitality, I would have to disagree. Tanya is a gifted teacher and servant, but she does not have a strong gift of hospitality. A person with the gift of hospitality would have been the one at the door to greet and possibly hug everyone as they arrived, making sure they felt welcomed, accepted and comfortable. Tanya, however, was focused on two things: making sure all of the work was done, and making sure her teaching was ready. Thankfully, Tanya is also a delegator and had a group of people prepared to meet and greet. The event was a huge success!

My daughter Lily has the gift of hospitality. Weeks before any major event takes place, she is making preparations for all those who will be coming. Lily loves to create custom placemats every Thanksgiving. She spends tons of time making sure they accurately reflect the person's nature. She wants everyone to feel special. When guests arrive for a party, Lily is in the driveway to welcome them in. When people leave, she walks them to the car.

Kids who have the gift of hospitality are nurturing. These kids are great at welcoming people and making sure that everyone feels better when they arrive. These kids care about things like atmosphere and environment. If your kid has this gift, he or she will often use things like notes, cards and flowers to bring a sense of welcome and belonging into someone's life.

Your child might have the gift of hospitality if you notice these patterns:

- He/she likes to provide an environment where people feel valued and cared for.
- When meeting new people, he/she helps them feel welcomed.
- Creates a safe and comfortable setting where relationships can develop.
- Seeks ways to connect people together in meaningful relationships.
- Sets people at ease in unfamiliar surroundings.
- Reaches out to the outcast.
- Is friendly.
- Organizes tea parties and other types of events with an attention to people-oriented detail.

If your kids have any or all of the gifts of serving, they will be the hands and feet of the church. Servants multiply the Kingdom by coming alongside others, giving their resources, doing the things that no one likes to do, and helping others accomplish the task at hand. Servants get things done.

Note
1. Blue Letter Bible, s.v. *diakonia*. http://www.blueletterbible.org/lang/lexicon/lexicon.cfm?strongs=G1248.

7

Bringers of Mercy

The Gifts of Compassion

*The pastor said if we wanted to pray and see people healed
we should come forward. So I did.*

FIVE-YEAR-OLD BRADEN'S RESPONSE
TO WHY HE WANDERED OFF

Spiritual Gifts Category 3: Compassion
Encouragement, Healing, Mercy

Most humans do everything in their power to remove suffering
from their lives. This is why compassion is so radical. Compassion
is the desire to suffer with others, to enter into their pain with understanding, empathy and hope.

Compassion is a key element of love's expression. It is the glue
of deep human connectedness. Compassion is the fuel for world-
changing and Kingdom-bringing actions. The heart of the gospel
is compassionate in nature. When Jesus gave up heaven's glory to
enter into our pain by taking it on His shoulders, He was living
out compassion. Jesus saw our pain and stepped into it. He identified with us in all of our sufferings.

Who, being in very nature God, did not consider equality
with God something to be grasped, but made himself

nothing, taking the very nature of a servant, being made in
human likeness (Phil. 2:6-7).

This compassionate act, like all compassionate acts, had the
power to heal! Because compassion mimics an act of Christ's nature, it has an inherent, God-infused power to bring healing.

Here's what I mean. When Jesus became sin on the cross, all of
the world's pain was heaved upon Him. He became our pain; He entered into it. After Jesus endured the pain of the cross—not just physical pain, but also the emotional and spiritual pain of separation
from God because of our sin—the result was that we were healed. Jesus' act of love and compassion lavished spiritual healing upon
"whoever believes in Him." Healing is also released in many ways
through our acts of compassion. If you want to have a ministry that
adds to the healing of others, pray for the gift of compassion.

God made him who had no sin to be sin for us, so that in
him we might become the righteousness of God (2 Cor. 5:21).

He himself bore our sins in his body on the tree, so that
we might die to sins and live for righteousness; by his
wounds you have been healed (1 Pet. 2:24).

When we look at Scripture, we see that Jesus healed others as
a result of His compassion for their needs:

When Jesus landed and saw a large crowd, he had compassion on them and healed their sick (Matt. 14:14).

Jesus had compassion on them and touched their eyes. Immediately they received their sight and followed him
(Matt. 20:34).

Filled with compassion, Jesus reached out his hand and
touched the man. "I am willing," he said. "Be clean!"
(Mark 1:41).

Kids who walk in the gifts of compassion—encouragement, healing, mercy—are healers. I'm not saying that they will see the lame walk, but they might. If you identify gifts of compassion within your child, you will want to help furnish opportunities for them to respond to the needs that touch their hearts. A great way to do this is to ask them what they want to do about a certain situation that arises. If they don't have any ideas, you might want to present some options. This could be an opportunity to visit a local home for the aged or a children's hospital. Discipling your son or daughter to lay hands on and pray for the sick is another fantastic idea. If you don't know how to do that, I am sure there are people in your church who do. Ask to ride shotgun with them, as a family, on their next trip to pray for the sick.

Encouragement

The spiritual gift of *encouragement* is the ability to strengthen another person through words or perhaps your physical presence. Encouragers bring comfort and healing to others. They spur them on.

Lucy, our three-year-old, has the gift of encouragement. Lucy is an emotional cheerleader. One of her goals in life is to make a person feel edified and supported.

I first recognized this gift in Lucy on a neighborhood walk. Like kids do, Lily challenged her sister to a race. Obviously, a three-year-old was not going to beat a third-grader in a test of speed.

Lily was kind enough to give Lucy a head start. The race began like many others, with the shout of "Go!" What was different about this race was that when Lily overtook Lucy, Lucy began to cheer, "Go, Lily! Go, Lily!"

Since I am a playground dad at Lily's school, I have seen a lot of races like this. Usually one kid starts crying, or quits, when he or she begins to lose the race; not Lucy. As a matter of fact, when Lily crossed the finish line, relegating Lucy to the loser's podium, Lucy exclaimed with delight, "We all win!" Lily tried to convince Lucy that she had actually lost the race, but Lucy was having none

of it. This is because if you are a true encourager, when someone
else on your team or in your family does well, you perceive it as all
having won. What a great perspective on life!

Here is another email from our small-group friends Rick and
Destiny. This time it relates to their son Jude's gift of encouragement:

> Jude definitely has the gift of encouragement. Recently, a
> dad approached me and said that his first-grade boy was
> sad he had to wear an eye patch and glasses to school. He
> didn't want the kids to make fun of him. When he walked
> in the door, Jude noticed the boy was nervous and uncom-
> fortable with the other kids' questions, so he took him
> aside and showed him his own glasses. He told the boy it
> was okay and not that big of a deal.

This is such a cool story!

Your kid might have the spiritual gift of encouragement if
you recognize the following pattern:

- Teachers mention how well liked he or she is by class-
  mates. This is because encouragers are some of the most
  well-liked people in the world. Who does not like some-
  one who makes them feel better?
- Tells others they were missed after they return from an
  absence.
- Verbally cheers others on.
- Tends to see the best in others.
- Is less critical or negative than other kids.
- Gives well-timed encouragement.
- Is a motivator of others.
- After hearing of someone's accomplishments they say
  things like, "That's great!" or "Good job!"
- Uses appropriate physical touch (hugs, arm around
  shoulder) to encourage someone who is down.
- Encourages you.

Healing

The spiritual gift of *healing* is the ability to be used as a conduit for God to deliver supernatural healing and wholeness to another.

The first kid I ever met with the gift of healing was when I was a youth pastor in Newport Beach, California. One of the pastors in our area had a five-year-old son, let's call him Braden, who walked powerfully in a number of spiritual gifts. One of these gifts was healing.

One time, during an evening church service, we had a time where people could come forward for healing prayer. Others in the congregation were invited to come down as well and pray for those at the front. While people were flowing down the aisles, Braden's parents noticed that he had disappeared. Somehow he had taken off while their eyes were closed.

They looked all around, only to find him at the altar praying over a man who had a lingering illness. When asked later why he went down to the front to pray, Braden responded, "The pastor said if we wanted to pray and see people healed, we should come forward. So I did."

Here again is another example of where we might have a tendency to unintentionally hinder our kids. For some reason, we just don't believe that things like healing prayer are available to our children.

Here's the great part of the story. The man that Braden prayed for was healed! This actually makes scriptural sense, as healing is tied to faith, and Jesus made it clear that kids have a type of faith we should all try to emulate.

> Some men brought to him a paralytic, lying on a mat. *When Jesus saw their faith*, he said to the paralytic, "Take heart, son; your sins are forgiven" (Matt. 9:2, emphasis added).

> When Jesus saw this, he was indignant. He said to them, "Let the little children come to me, and *do not hinder them,* for the kingdom of God belongs to such as these. I tell you the truth, anyone who will not receive the kingdom of God

like a little child will never enter it (Mark 10:14-15, emphasis added).

Your child might have the gift of healing if you have witnessed the following pattern:

- He or she has prayed for someone and seen the person healed.
- When hearing of a person's illness, he/she wants to pray about it.
- Often remembers ill people during family prayer times.
- Makes faith-filled statements about God's healing ability.
- Physically comforts, hugs or touches a person who is sick or hurting. This is because the laying on of hands is part of God's healing equation in many cases. I have found that people with the gift of healing do this naturally.
- Is not uncomfortable or scared when going into hospitals.
- Has a deep sense of compassion.

Mercy

The spiritual gift of *mercy* starts with a heart for the hurting and the outcast. Mercy shows its fruit in taking action to meet the needs of the hurting and despondent.

The opening section of this chapter about compassion could easily be posted here. Compassion is a form of mercy. People with the gift of mercy seek to care for victims of unjust treatment. They want to see God's love and grace released to all broken people. Merciful kids will often reach out to the outcast. Like Jesus, they will go toward the broken. These kids are sensitive to others' pain and unjust treatment.

As you know, we consider blessed those who have persevered. You have heard of Job's perseverance and have seen what the Lord finally brought about. The Lord is full of compassion and mercy (Jas. 5:11).

Kids with a gift of mercy will tend to be forgiving and less judgmental than most. Mercy does, after all, supersede judgment. Kids with the gift of mercy will reflect this scriptural truth.

Mercy triumphs over judgment! (Jas. 2:13).

Here is a quick story from friends who think they are seeing the gift of compassion in their child.

Roxy is especially sensitive to sarcasm or even teasing. If we watch a movie about a child getting bullied or being scorned, she often cries and leaves the room. If someone is trying to read a story in class and another child laughs, Roxy will cry at the meanness of it. She doesn't like me to tell stories of my "most embarrassing" moments, as it makes her too uncomfortable.

Your kid might have the gift of mercy if he/she shows this pattern of behavior:

- Cries or expresses emotion when others are expressing their pain in words or tears.
- Responds to the illness of a pet in a very caring manner.
- Includes the outcast in games or sporting events.
- Sticks up for or might even get involved in a fight at school for the sake of another.
- Asks lots of questions after witnessing someone being mistreated.
- Seeks ways to alleviate people's discomfort.
- Is consistently kind.
- Tends to look out for younger siblings.
- Carries others' burdens long after others have moved on.
- Gives others second chances.
- Forgives others more easily than most people do.

8

Kids of Understanding

The Gifts of Understanding

If you seek God for your future, you believe in prophecy.

Spiritual Gifts Category 4: Understanding
**Discernment, Interpretation of Tongues, Tongues, Knowledge,
Intercession/Prayer, Wisdom, Prophecy**

I recently spent time with a friend who was explaining to me how
God communicates with us today. His point was that God has given
us the Bible, and all that we need to know for living and decision-
making is found in those pages. My friend believes that as long as we
don't break any of God's ordinances as found in the pages of Scripture, we can make whatever decisions we want, and God does not
direct us with thoughts, dreams, impressions or a gentle inner voice.

How we hear from God and communicate His message to hu-
mankind is another one of those hot buttons that puts you in a theological camp. On one side, we have those people, like my friend,
who believe that as long as we live within the bounds of God's Word,
we don't need to seek God for further revelation. On the other side,
or camp, are believers who feel that God is always speaking fresh
words of revelation to them and to the rest of His Church. These are
believers who might tell you that they have a special word from the
LORD for you or that God laid a verse on their hearts. These followers of Christ hear God in the supermarket, while watching TV or
perhaps in dreams and visions.

I fall somewhere in the middle of these two camps. I am a pastor within the Calvary Chapel movement. If you are not familiar with Calvary Chapel, it began with the Jesus people, the hippies who loved Jesus.

Back in the 1970s, God was on the move in a fresh wave of revival. Chuck Smith, the founder of Calvary Chapel, was stuck between a rock and a hard place. As a biblical conservative, Pastor Chuck was not inclined toward many of the manifestations of God's Spirit that he was seeing among his new congregants. On the other hand, lots of people were being saved as a result, and he was not a man to hinder a work of God.

If you have followed Calvary Chapel during the last few decades, you might know that they have tried to focus on maintaining the biblical balance of God's revealed truth as seen in the pages of Scripture, while allowing for a full palate of the gifts. In his book *Charisma vs. Charismania,* Pastor Chuck addresses this tension.[1] While the book is a bit dated these days, it still does a great job of speaking to this issue. If you are currently in the midst of this tension between whether the charismatic gifts are for today or not, you might want to pick up this book via one of the online bookstores.

I am a person who hears God in all sorts of places. I often get a thought or word picture that seems to have the fragrance of God on it. My only requirement when I hear these words is to test the message. Does the message stand up to scriptural truth? Does the message reflect the history and message of believers who have gone before me? Does it stand to reason and what my personal experience to this point in life and ministry has shown me?[2]

Because of this, Calvary Chapel has been a great fit for my family and me. Sure, there are plenty of people who would love to see our movement toss out the more charismatic gifts altogether. Others long for us to dive deeper into this arena and have a desire that all the gifts would be a regular part of the weekly service.

In the end, I am very content as to where we have landed. You know a work of God by its fruit. Yes, we allow the gifts, but they do not define us. If we, as a movement, continue on in the direction we are heading, the legacy of Calvary Chapel will be known as a Bible-teaching, soul-winning, discipling church filled with God's power and gifts.

Communicating to His Peeps

The "understanding" spiritual gifts are all about communication. Each of them is intended to act as a line of contact between God, His people and a lost world. What is God saying now, and what does He want us to do about it?

One thing is true of each of these gifts. Like every good and perfect gift that comes from God, they have been entrusted to flawed people. See the verses below that speak of this tension.

Whether you are dealing with the understanding of a particular text of Scripture in a conservative church, or interpreting a tongue within a charismatic congregation, they can both be mishandled and misspoken. Just because you stand on a *sola scriptura* (scripture only) understanding of hearing from God, you still have to decide what is the right understanding of each Scripture. Just as we can be misdirected through tongues, who would not argue that the same danger is fully present when dealing with God's Word? Cults are a great example of this.

For we know in part and we prophesy in part (1 Cor. 13:9).

Every good and perfect gift is from above, coming down from the Father of the heavenly lights, who does not change like shifting shadows (Jas. 1:17).

As we move through this particular set of gifts, I want to reiterate that I am not trying to convince you of their merits. There are lots of amazing believers who are way smarter and more godly than me, who stand on opposite sides of these particular gifts. My hope is that God will meet you in whatever tradition you reside and make you aware of His equipping within your children.

Remember, this book is more about discipling your kids into ministry than about changing your denominational stance on the spiritual gifts. With that said, I will do my best to share what I believe God has shown me in regard to His ability and method in speaking to His kids.

Remember, this book is more about discipling your kids into ministry than about changing your denominational stance on the spiritual gifts.

Discernment

The spiritual gift of *discernment* allows the believer to rapidly see to the core of an issue and know the truth. This could relate to doctrinal error, a ministry decision, relational and spiritual issues, and so on.

When you come to a fork in the road, you need to use discernment to know which way to go. Discernment is what keeps us within the bounds of God's truth. It also keeps us safe from harm.

While all of us have a degree of discernment, some believers have a heightened sense of it and fall into the category of being spiritually gifted with discernment. I have walked in this gift for many years now, and I depend on it when meeting with people. This applies to bringing new people onto our ministry team or managing our benevolence ministry funds for the poor. As sad as it is, there are many people who make it their practice to try to steal money from the church by pretending to be a person in need. The gift of discernment regularly helps me guard and protect not only God's resources, but also His flock.

If your kid has the gift of discernment, he or she will have more raw material to work with when it comes to decision-making. This is not to say that your child will make right decisions every time, but that he or she has a special, God-given sensitivity to see and discern things beyond what most people recognize.

Birthday Presents and Discernment

Last year on my birthday, I witnessed our eight-year-old, Lily, use God-given discernment. Over the last year or so, I have begun to think this is a legitimate spiritual gift in her life and walk of faith.

Because I love the fantasy books of J. R. R. Tolkien and reading about the history of the Middle Ages, I've collected some really ornate, painted toys. There are dragons, men with axes, and knights in fighting poses. These figures are displayed in a massive battle scene on a shelf in my office.

Before my fortieth birthday, I decided that I needed a new villain for the tableau. I came across a very dark-looking figure on horseback that I thought would fit in perfectly. I used my iPhone to send a picture of it to my wife and requested it as a birthday gift. However, as I sent the text, I got the impression that I should not ask for this particular figurine. I'm not saying it was in the sin category, but for some reason, there was a check in my spirit. It was just a little dark.

On my birthday, as I was opening my gifts, I got to the one that looked like it would be the beastly addition to the collection. But when I opened it, there was a white knight on a regal-looking steed instead of what I expected. While it was cool, it was not what I had asked for. When I inquired why, Lily told me that when she got to the cash register with her mother, God spoke to her heart and told her not to buy it for me. What she heard was exactly what God had told me.

While there are a lot of possible explanations for Lily's experience, I feel that it was an act of spiritual discernment. Lily had a decision to make in regard to the gift she was going to give me. God helped Lily discern that what I wanted was not what God wanted for me. Thankfully, Lily was more willing to listen to God about it than I was.

When this happened, I paused in opening my birthday presents to affirm Lily. I told her that what she did in obedience to what she heard resonated with what God had spoken to my heart. I let her know that her spiritual voice mattered to us as a family. I told her that I thought this might be the inkling of the spiritual gift of discernment in her, but that we would have to continue to check the fruit of her life to see if that was the case.

Affirm Them in Their Hearing

When we don't affirm our children in their spiritual hearing, or other gifts, we might be setting them up for some major failures in the future. If we disregard our children's sensitivity to what God is saying to them in the quiet of their hearts, they will begin to doubt if they can hear from God.

If kids have been conditioned to believe that those early promptings were not of value, they will begin to disregard them. As a parent, you have a tremendous ability to shape your children's future by letting them know that you value the voice of God within them. This means that when they process something they have understood or heard from God, you take them seriously and help them process it. This is the difference between provision-and-protection parenting, and parental discipleship.

If your kids are like mine, they sometimes point out things in your life that need work and redemption. Often they are discerning things that God has shown them. My tendency is to tell my children why they are wrong and to defend myself rather than receive what they have shared and begin to pray over it. One example of this is when Lily told me that I was being too harsh in my discipline of her. She had prayed about it and then come to talk to me.

She was right, and God had already shared this with me. Unfortunately, instead of receiving what she said, I defended myself. I made her think she was wrong and that I was justified. Later, I went back to her and apologized. I told her that she was right, and God had said the same thing to me. I affirmed her ability to hear from God correctly and told her that she was always free to share these things with me.

By taking seriously what our kids spiritually discern, and by valuing their input, we teach our sons and daughters that we value their spiritual voice. When we discover they were right in their understanding, we have an opportunity to edify them in their ability to hear from their heavenly Father. This will pay massive dividends when they are making decisions far from the confines of our parental protection. It might even save their lives.

If your child has the spiritual gift of discernment, he or she might display the following traits:

- He or she can read a person's character shortly after meeting them.
- Is hard to fool.
- He or she might be the first of your kids to dispel the Santa or Easter Bunny myths.
- Can recognize God's truth and identify it as such.
- Might be more tentative than most before rushing in to a new situation.
- Is aware of spiritual attack or God's presence in a place.
- Is aware of when the devil is up to something. This could be in the way he/she processes night terrors, which is common with many believing children.
- Has a strong sense of what God would have him or her do or not do.
- Makes decisions based on internal and external processing.
- Is perceptive and sensitive.

Tongues and the Interpretation of Tongues

The gift of *tongues* is the ability to speak in a God-given spiritual language that is for the purposes of edifying the Church, personal prayer, or being understood by nonbelievers for the purpose of their salvation. *Interpretation of tongues* is the ability to understand and communicate in common language the meaning of a tongue given by another member of the Body of Christ.

The Scriptures show us a few usages of the gift of tongues. Tongues are used for the salvation of others. Tongues are also used to communicate revelation to God's people and for prayer. Here is a quick scriptural look at these scenarios.

Tongues for the Purpose of Salvation

"Tongues, then, are a sign, not for believers but for unbelievers; prophecy, however, is for believers, not for unbelievers" (1 Cor. 14:22).

This usage of tongues was as a sign to unbelievers that would cause them to believe in the gospel message of Jesus Christ as their Messiah. We see this displayed in Acts 2:

> People of all languages recognized the miracle of supernatural translation. This sign led many to a salvific knowledge of Christ. "[Both Jews and converts to Judaism]; Cretans and Arabs—we hear them declaring the wonders of God in our own tongues!" (Acts 2:11).

Tongues as Revelation to Believers

Since believers are already in the Church, they don't need a "sign" leading to salvation. Because of this, tongues have a different purpose for them. Tongues in the church setting are meant as a method of communication. When God wants to communicate a unique message to a certain group of His people or particular church, He might choose to do so through the spiritual gift of tongues.

When a tongue is given within the community of believers, it must always be followed with interpretation. The body of believers must accept this interpretation and see it as true to Scripture. Paul speaks about the effective use of tongues in 1 Corinthians 14:6-13.

> Now, brothers, if I come to you and speak in tongues, what good will I be to you, unless I bring you some revelation or knowledge or prophecy or word of instruction? Even in the case of lifeless things that make sounds, such as the flute or harp, how will anyone know what tune is being played unless there is a distinction in the notes? Again, if the trumpet does not sound a clear call, who will get ready for battle? So it is with you. Unless you speak intelligible words with your tongue, how will anyone know what you are saying? You will just be speaking into the air. Undoubtedly there are all sorts of languages in the world, yet none of them is without mean-

ing. If then I do not grasp the meaning of what someone is saying, I am a foreigner to the speaker, and he is a foreigner to me. So it is with you. Since you are eager to have spiritual gifts, try to excel in gifts that build up the church. For this reason anyone who speaks in a tongue should pray that he may interpret what he says.[3]

Tongues as Prayer

The final scriptural usage of tongues is in the area of prayer.[4] Paul mentions this type of prayer in 1 Corinthians 14:4. This is a supernatural form of prayer that relies on God's Spirit praying through you. It often happens when people do not know how to pray or are dealing with some major situation in their life. I have experienced this form of prayer in many emergency rooms. It is also often used in regard to intercession for a person's soul or when dealing with spiritual oppression.

> For if I pray in a tongue, my spirit prays, but my mind is unfruitful (1 Cor. 14:14).

Here is a story that my friend Stacy emailed me about a recent time when her son interpreted a tongue:

> One night while putting our four-year-old and six-year-old to bed, my husband and I found ourselves praying for our younger son's health. He had been pretty sick, and we were praying a usual bedtime blessing with a little extra request for God to heal his virus. As we were praying for him, we began to pray quietly in tongues, not a usual practice around the kids, but we felt the Spirit prompting, so we went for it. As we prayed, our oldest on the bunk above us said plainly, "I know what you guys are saying." Very surprised (probably because of how rarely interpretations are offered), we asked him to tell us. He said with confidence, "You're saying, 'God, send that sickness right out of Ramón, and heal him.'" He continued, as we prayed, to

offer interpretations that resonated perfectly with our praying hearts.

I have personally seen the effective and scripturally accurate use of the gift of tongues in a few children and have met many adults who said they began speaking in tongues as children. Maybe you or your kids are one of them.

Your kid might have the gift of tongues or interpretation of tongues if you see this pattern:

- He or she has interpreted a tongue after it was given in the larger church setting.
- He/she speaks in tongues.
- He/she prays in tongues.

Knowledge

The spiritual gift of *knowledge* is twofold. It is the ability to grasp deep scriptural truth, and it is also a spiritual insight into particular situations.

As a teacher of God's Word, I am often affirmed in my gift of knowledge. People will tell me that they appreciate the way I recognize aspects in Scripture that others often miss.

Some might categorize this as a manifestation of the teaching gift. I would disagree. Teaching is the ability to relay knowledge to another. The gift of knowledge is the ability to grasp or understand a truth of God. Thus, one can have the gift of knowledge and be a very poor teacher. This is not to say that many teachers operate in both a teaching and knowledge gift.

A word of knowledge is also when God shares with a believer supernatural insight into a person, situation or event, which they could not possibly have known in the natural. Many Christian counselors walk in this gifting. Oftentimes, God will give them just the right question to ask. I experience this gift most often when praying for people. Usually while I am praying, I will get a thought or impression about the person or situation I am praying for.

When this happens, rather then saying, "God told me this or that," I will instead just ask questions in line with what I think God has revealed to me: "Have you ever struggled with addiction?" or "Were you raised in an abusive environment?" As I have stepped out in sensitivity, wisdom and faith, I have seen these words and understandings hit the mark and open doors to greater healing. With that said, I have also gotten it wrong. The key is doing everything in love and with an understanding that you might be off the mark.

One of the reasons people struggle with this type of revelation is that it is so often abused. If you have spent any time with the "Thus sayeth the LORD" crowd, then you know what I mean. I have seen too many people misuse this gift to keep count.

Sharing knowledge given to you in the Spirit, whether in a sermon or with a person you are praying with, is always to be done with care and caution. This is especially true if you are stepping out into uncharted territory.

Here is a story from some close friends who have experienced the gift of knowledge with their children:

Since the age of three, our son has repeatedly made profound statements or proclamations about someone or something that is far beyond his years. We now have identified many of these as "words of knowledge."

The first [word of knowledge] I can remember was when a family we are very close to was entering a severe trial and testing of their faith. At the core of their family's trial was the felt need for peace—not just an end to the trial, but a deep, abiding, life-changing peace in their relationships with one another. While eating breakfast one morning, my son said to me, "Mama, peace is coming to the Robinsons."

It came out of nowhere, and no previous context would even have spurred the thought to his mind that morning. As he spoke it, my spirit received it as the truth from God. I called my dear friend that day and left her a message relaying the word from my son, confident that it was indeed from God. She held on to that message, literally, in her voice-mail box for over two years. And I can stand to testify right now that that peace, while long-awaited and tirelessly fought for, has come to the Robinsons. Amen. [Her son had just turned three when he spoke the word of knowledge.]

If your child has the gift of knowledge, you might notice the following pattern:

- He/she says profound things beyond his or her years.
- Has uncanny insights into the lives of others.
- Grasps deep biblical truths.
- The truth or understandings he or she relates come to fruition.
- Has confidence in what he or she feels he or she is hearing from God.
- Will convey messages that resonate with your spirit.
- Reveals things about events that you know are true but he or she would have no way of knowing.
- Has unique insights into Scripture.

Intercession/Prayer

The gift of *intercession/prayer* is the ability to pray at length and with effectiveness. Intercessors stand in the gap. In the book of Ezekiel, we see God looking for someone who is willing to stand in the gap:

> I looked for a man among them who would build up the wall and stand before me in the gap on behalf of the land so I would not have to destroy it, but I found none (Ezek. 22:30).

God was looking for someone who would take on the spiritual battle of intercession. What this verse is saying to anyone who will believe is that we humans have the ability to change the course of human events through our prayers.

Matthew 16:19 talks about this ability when Jesus gives Peter (as well as all other believers) keys to the kingdom of heaven. These keys have the ability to bind up and loose events and consequences, not only on the earth but also in heaven itself. Since there is no age limit in the kingdom of God, this applies to your kids as well.

> I will give you the keys of the kingdom of heaven; whatever you bind on earth will be bound in heaven, and whatever you loose on earth will be loosed in heaven (Matt. 16:19).

While we understand that all believers have this ability, God has called some to go beyond what most believers will ever experience in the area of faith-filled prayer. These gap-standers are the fuel of much of the Kingdom work we see around us every day. I believe that without this army of prayer warriors around the world, the encroaching darkness we are experiencing today would be far greater.

I can honestly say that I am alive today because of some very powerful intercessors. Back in the 1980s when I left home, I quickly became entangled in the world and all it had to offer. As I look back now, I know with absolute certainty that God rescued me on numerous occasions due to the faithfulness of a handful of my mom's prayer team! If your kids are in a similar situation as I have described about my early life, find some intercessors and release the hounds of heaven!

The following story was sent to me from the wife of a local pastor. This story gives an example of what this type of gifting in kids might look like:

> We recently stumbled into a prolonged and Spirit-filled prayer session with my two sons before bedtime (they are three and five). It began simply as my husband started praying for health in our family. As he prayed, my oldest son just began to jump right in with him. Before long, all three were praying out about tons of different things on

their hearts. The prayers that stood out to my husband were from my oldest son as he said, "God, please free my father from the fear of getting sick." As he prayed, it was like someone hit the nail on the head and the fear was broken. Then he began to pray for the world. He prayed for China, because he had heard on the news that they weren't getting along with the U.S. Then he prayed for soldiers in Iraq and Afghanistan, and in particular, for the Captains— that they would be godly leaders in battle.

Your kid might have the spiritual gift of intercession/prayer if you notice the following pattern:

- You catch him/her praying when you are not looking.
- He/she offers to pray for others without prompting.
- Is attentive during prayer.
- Inquires about prayers you have prayed in the past to know the results.
- Believes that prayer works.
- Talks about prayer.
- Asks to be prayed for.
- When praying, tends to pray longer than most kids.
- Displays emotion during prayer. Might cry for someone when praying.

Wisdom

The spiritual gift of *wisdom* allows a believer to make accurate and well-timed decisions. Wisdom incorporates insight into what is true and right with an understanding of how to implement that knowledge into action.

The Scripture says that David's son Solomon was the wisest man to ever walk the earth. Solomon could see to the core of an issue. Solomon could discern the truth. That's what wisdom is. Wisdom is light and truth, and it has the ability to create straight paths for living.

I will do what you have asked. I will give you a wise and discerning heart, so that there will never have been anyone like you, nor will there ever be (1 Kings 3:12).

I guide you in the way of wisdom and lead you along straight paths (Prov. 4:11).

Wise people are sought after. When the challenges of life overtake us, we often turn to those who are wise for counsel. Believers with the gift of wisdom help guide the church in the way it should go. Kids with this gifting are often concise when communicating and have a high regard for justice and fairness. What follows is a story from our friend Sherry. I think Sherry is onto something in realizing that spiritual gifting can sometimes be found in places you wouldn't expect.

At this point, Chum (nickname) has the gift of arguing. I know some people get paid very well in that field. At this age (6), we are still trying to break that spirit down. As a parent, I don't want to just view this characteristic with negativity because it can be difficult to deal with.

Chum is strong, bold and loyal; she comes out swingin' and asks questions later. She has a strong sense of fairness and unfairness! These characteristics can manifest themselves in unsavory ways when kids are young. But that's not to say that they can't develop into "savory" traits later. But again, I'm unclear on what defines "gift."

Because the apostle Paul did not write a separate book on what spiritual gifts always look like, we are left to figure out a lot of it on our own. I would say that with spiritual gifts, the Bible is more of a compass than a road map. The Bible tells us what the spiritual gifts are, but it does not give a laundry list of how to accurately define these gifts in all people. We are left to seek, explore and test. Obviously, that is the approach of this book. By now, I hope that you are being equipped and released to start exploring your kids' spiritual gifts.

In the email you just read, Chum seems to have some of the raw material of wisdom. While arguing is not always a great trait, it can point to a person who wants to get to the bottom of things to find truth or the best answer. Chum also has a sense of what is just and unjust. Is this not what wise judges are concerned with?

While I can't assuredly say that Chum has the gift of wisdom, she at least is displaying enough of the gifting to begin to test for it. One way to do that would be to offer Chum more opportunities to make decisions for herself. As parents, we don't often do this well. Instead, we love to give wisdom. My challenge to Steve and Sherry will be to create opportunities for Chum to make choices that will develop her ability to do the next right thing.

Another way to do this is by presenting real-life issues to your kids to see what they would do. Perhaps there is a problem at school where the leadership is seeking a solution. Maybe you have a family issue that needs to be resolved. Why not ask your kids what they think about it, and see if their answers display wisdom. If they do, you might be dealing with a spiritually gifted wise kid.

The *word of wisdom* gift is sometimes seen as a charismatic gift, but it often flies under the radar in conservative churches. Many mainline Christians will offer a word of wisdom in the same way that a charismatic or Pentecostal believer would step out in offering a revelation of knowledge or wisdom that comes straight from the Holy Spirit. But instead of saying they got it from God, they will just wrap it in the form of sound advice that has come out of a time of prayer. They don't know it, but they are actually displaying a charismatic understanding of this gift. Having grown up in a conservative denomination myself, I can look back in time and see many instances when conservative believers walked in a charismatic fashion. They just didn't know they were doing it.

Your child might have the gift of wisdom if you see this pattern:

- He/she applies spiritual truth to life situations. This means that your child references God's truth from the Bible when making decisions.

- Doesn't freeze or move too quickly when making a decision.
- When a person has a problem, he or she guides the person to the best biblical solution.
- Friends ask him or her for solutions.
- His/her decisions turn out well.
- He/she intuits correct answers to complicated problems.
- He/she is comfortable with balancing many possible solutions without being overwhelmed.
- He/she is a truth seeker.
- Has a heart for justice and fairness.
- Likes to hear both sides of a story before making a decision.
- Doesn't make lots of quick, impetuous decisions.

Prophecy

The spiritual gift of *prophecy* is the ability to understand God's future purposes and plans for His people.

I think we would all agree that God leads His people. Back in the day, this was done through God's ordained leaders, such as the prophets and judges who communicated God's revelation. These men and women were forecasters of the future. They didn't always understand all that God was communicating through them, but they were able to accurately see into God's plans for His people and their future and be God's mouthpiece.

Biblical prophecy through God's chosen prophets is set apart from other types of prophecy because it was perfect in its revelation. This type of prophecy is no longer available to us, as the canon of Scripture is closed, but there is a different form of prophecy that is. Now, *every* believer has God's recorded Word (the Bible) as a blueprint for God's general will, and the Holy Spirit living within for guidance in specific situations. Because God guides His people through His Word and through the Holy Spirit, He will often clue us in to more than general revelation and show us what His plans are for our individual lives or for the future of a particular church or people group. I would say that if you seek God for your future, you believe in prophecy.

God is not limited in how He unfolds our future path. Sometimes a timely Scripture will give you a hint into God's coming plans for you. Other times, you might have a dream or be approached by a friend who feels that God has given them some insight for your future. Maybe your child will speak about the future with a sense of authority that resonates with your soul.

With that said, I must address the tension between those that see prophecy as forthtelling vs. foretelling. The following article addresses this issue:

> The verb "prophesy" means "to speak before" (from Greek *pro,* before, and *phemi,* to speak). The gift includes both the idea of foretelling and forth telling, predicting the future and preaching. A prophet was God's mouthpiece: he spoke for God and gave His message. Sometimes that message was regarding the future. Other times it concerned the present, even the past, or simply doctrinal truth, but it was always God's message spoken forth.
>
> Some controversy arises at this point. Today's renewed interest and investigation of the spiritual gifts has seen many non-charismatics redefine the gift of prophecy. The Charismatics, of course, readily admit the revelatory nature of this gift and claim its operation today. Some modern non-charismatics have defined the gift in another way, resulting in an interpretation which allows the gift of prophecy today but not in its revelatory sense. They say that the gift of prophecy means only the ability to speak forth for God, to preach; it is not necessarily, they say, a revelatory gift, but the ability to preach the truth of God's Word with great power and insight.
>
> The issue can be stated in the form of two questions: (1) Is it Scripturally allowable to limit the gift to only forthtelling (as opposed to predictive prophecy)? and, (2) Is there in that forth telling nothing revelatory? That is, is it merely the ability to expound previously revealed truth? So the question to clarify at the outset is one of definitions.[5]

Testing Words of Prophecy

Karie and I have experienced these types of prophecy many times. My personal ministry calling, our family mission to Australia, even the birth of our daughters were all forecast to us before the fact.

For us, the proof has always come in the testing and the confirmation of these words. As I said, other believers forecast both of our children's births. This was risky for our friends, because we struggled with getting pregnant.

When it comes to receiving the prophetic for our lives, Karie and I have always employed the following plan of attack to determine the truth of it. First, does the word or message received violate scriptural truth in any way? If so, we toss it to the rubbish bin. Second, we begin to purify the word in prayer. Finally, we ask God to confirm it to us. We ask God to lead us in the truth.

Karie and I always hold the prophetic loosely. When I first started experiencing this gifting in my own life, I went overboard. I made a lot of unwise decisions as I tried to follow what were offered as prophetic words from God. After getting burned, and perhaps burning a few others in the process, I learned to be a lot wiser in the way I dealt with these words.

Over the years, I have had hundreds of words given to me through other believers. Some have been repeated since I was 12 years old by many different people and in many different countries. These are not biblical prophecies, but rather spiritual words of hope, direction and encouragement that God has used to move me forward in my journey with Him.

As I have walked out my life of faith, I have seen many of these words fulfilled in my life; others never took root. One thing is true: I will never build a theology on these words; rather, I pray, listen, wait and test these possible whispers from God. The fulfillment of many of these words has greatly strengthened my faith.

Here is another story from our good friends Ryan and Stacy, who have experienced a prophetic gifting within their kids:

One time, we were in a season of prolonged waiting for a new home big enough for our growing family. After a couple years of waiting, praying and dying to our own plans and desires, the clock seemed to be running out on us. One night, it was Good Friday, and we were praying for the kids because there was a lightning storm that had frightened them. Out of nowhere my son said to me, "Mama, I'm going to need my BlueAzul (code for his security blanket) and my iguana, because we're moving soon." It was spoken like a fact, or even a promise. Within a week, we were contacted about a rental home that for months we had been fervently praying for. In less than 30 days, we had moved into that very house. (My son was three-and-a-quarter years old.)

Another time we experienced God speaking through our child was when we ran into some friends at church. When we walked away, our son said, "Mama, Anna [their only child] has a baby sister." I looked at him funny and said, "What? She doesn't have any sisters." He said, "Yes, her mommy has one in her tummy." By this time, I had learned to take note of these peculiar declarations. As with the others, there was no leading conversation on the topic, and they seemed to come out of nowhere. I held on to this one and waited to see what developed. Sure enough, within six weeks these friends announced they were pregnant! In fact, that day my son had said that to me, they hadn't even known yet. And when the baby was born, it was a girl!

Out of the Box

Okay, I know that stories like this are really far out of some of your spiritual boxes. That is fine. There is no scriptural mandate that you have to accept this. What I would hope that you would do is become more aware of your child's professions about God and His workings in the world. If you can do that, then this section is incredibly valuable to you, even if you can't accept some of its more fantastic illustrations. The point is this: *God directs and speaks to and through kids.*

Your kid might have the gift of prophecy if you see the following pattern:

- He/she offers up insights into the future that actually happen.
- Can see God's finished product in another person. Has the ability to see a person's potential that is not currently displayed.
- Has dreams about future events.
- Can see how certain Scripture pertains to future events.

Notes

1. Chuck Smith, *Charisma vs. Charismania* (Costa Mesa, CA: Word for Today, 1993).
2. This understanding reflects the Wesleyan Quadrilateral for processing God's messages and voice. See "Wesleyan Quadrilateral," Wikipedia.org. http://en.wikipedia.org/wiki/Wesleyan_Quadrilateral.
3. Note on verse 13: If a person were to interpret the tongue he or she has given, those receiving the tongue must accept it as true to Scripture for it to stand.
4. This gift has been left off of my spiritual gifts test, as it is a yes-or-no question that is easily discerned. If your kid has this gift, you will know it.
5. Fred G. Zaspel, "Prophets and Prophecy," biblicalstudies.com. http://www.biblical studies.com/bstudy/spiritualgifts/ch15.htm.

The Voice of Good News

The Gifts of Evangelism

*We are all missionaries. Wherever we go we either bring people
nearer to Christ or we repel them from Christ.*

ERIC LIDDELL

Spiritual Gifts Category 5: Salvation
Evangelism, Faith, Miracles, Tongues, Missions

When I first rededicated my life to Jesus at the age of 19, I was a
roving evangelist. I trolled the streets and piers of San Diego, California, looking for converts—once even leading an Elvis imperson-
ator to Christ while offering him a ride home. After introducing
him to Christ, he looked up and said, "Thank you, thank you very
much!" (Okay, he did not say that, but the rest of the story is true.)

Looking back, I am not sure if I had the gift of evangelism
or enthusiasm. Whatever it was, people were getting saved. In
the years that followed, I have become a professional Christian.
I get paid to be a believer. Now, instead of heading downtown
with a group of friends to reach pimps and prostitutes with the
good news of Jesus Christ, I go to conferences held in nice hotels
and discuss culturally relevant ways to evangelize a modern and
tech-savvy culture.

As putrid as that sounds, it is what often happens when we spend too much time thinking about God and His Matthew 28:19-20 calling to us rather than being His hands, feet and voice to a hurting world. Trust me, I'm doing my best to recapture what I have lost. Thankfully, somewhere in the far reaches of my soul there is a crazy 19-year-old, fresh off of drugs and crazy in love with Jesus, who is screaming at the top of his lungs for me to remember those days.

All of the evangelism gifts listed in this chapter have a unique stake in the winning of souls. While not all of them are always used for this purpose—miracles, for instance—each of them are used to turn people from darkness to the light of faith.

Evangelism

The spiritual gift of *evangelism* is the ability to boldly share the message of salvation in a way that is clear, concise and effective. Evangelists not only share the gospel, but they also see people make a decision for Christ.

I'm sure that we are all pretty clear on the fact that when we get to heaven, we won't be able to pull out the old "I just didn't have the gift of evangelism" card. We are all called to not only share the gospel but also to disciple others into a sound and sustainable faith. As a parent, your primary audience is your kids. Isn't it funny how we all seem to have the gift of evangelism when it comes to reaching them? We all make a concerted effort to make sure our kids know Jesus. This is because we care about them. Think about how the world would change if we could transfer this same kind of care and concern to everyone around us. The world and the devil would not have a chance.

In 1979, while on her knees in front of an old tube television, my mother knelt with her hand on the screen as Billy Graham prayed a prayer of salvation. When we think about evangelism, our minds move to the Billy Grahams, the John Wesleys and the Luis Palaus of this world. These men, and many women like them, seem to have a unique ability to call others from the gates of hell.

I am convinced that one of the most powerful evangelistic witnesses in the world today is children who believe in Jesus. Have you ever met a child evangelist? I have met many. These are the kids who invite all of their friends to church, talk about Jesus at inconvenient times and often embarrass their parents.

Our friends Sean and Lisa are parents to one such evangelist. Remember nine-year-old Jaden from earlier in this book? Jaden can't stop telling everyone she can about the good news of Jesus. Jaden is not only an evangelist, but an apologist as well. She gets into some really good debates with friends at school, often coming home, seeking answers and heading back out with new fodder. Other friends of ours have received calls from parents asking them to call off the dogs, upset that their child is hearing about hell and the love of Jesus on the playground.

Because most parents don't know how to encourage or shepherd this gift, they might ignore it or pass it off as cute, instead of leaning in and helping their child develop their calling as an evangelist. This could easily be done by reading accounts of some of the great evangelists to their kids or spending time praying and dreaming with their child about ways to reach their friends. Instead, the spark often dies out because the early kindling of evangelistic fervor was never given more fuel for its fire.

Your child might have the gift of evangelism if you notice the following pattern:

- He/she is unafraid to speak with others about Jesus.
- Shares the gospel with friends.
- You have been called by other parents and asked to speak to your child about his/her witnessing practices.
- Has a burden for the lost.
- Is concerned about others going to hell, and, perhaps, asks questions about hell and salvation on a regular basis.
- Understands the consequence of hell in a deeper way than most kids.
- Has led a friend to Christ.
- Often invites friends to church.

• Can clearly articulate the gospel.
• Debates issues of the faith with unbelievers.
• Weeps over the lost.
• Experiences great joy when someone is saved.

Faith

The spiritual gift of *faith* is a strong belief in the promises and purposes of God. It is the ability to believe in things that are unseen. Hebrews describes faith as not just believing in things unseen, but being sure of those things:

> Now faith is being sure of what we hope for and certain of what we do not see (Heb. 11:1).

God-given faith is one of the most powerful forces in the universe. It has the power to not only move mountains but to change destinies. It is through faith that we are made eternally secure. Believers with the gift of faith often display that faith for the salvation of others; they believe God for the conversion of others' souls.

Faith is a form of spiritual power. This power is nothing that we create on our own, but rather it is released from God when we open up the channels of belief and trust.

Think of it this way: Faith is a conduit. All of God's power, the power to heal, save and accomplish all manner of things, is available to us in Him. Like a circuit breaker, this power is released when we get out of the way and flip the switch of faith. When we exhibit faith, it is the fullness of submission and trust in a God greater than ourselves. Faith is stepping out of our power and into His.

Whenever you get out of the natural and step out in believing faith, you are handing over the reins to God. When this happens, the channels are open for God to move and work in power. Faith, then, is more an act of submission than a work of the flesh. Get out of the way and believe in God's ability to work powerfully and you will be walking in faith. Watch and see what happens!

Understanding and Creating Lasting Childlike Faith

One of the miracles of creation is that God has hotwired us for faith. We are all born with the innate proclivity to believe without the need to have something proven to us. If Mommy or Daddy said it, kids most often believe it. The ability to receive the kingdom of God like a child is often called "childlike faith" and is a highly valued commodity in the kingdom of heaven. Here is what Jesus said about it:

> People were bringing little children to Jesus to have him touch them, but the disciples rebuked them. When Jesus saw this, he was indignant. He said to them, "Let the little children come to me, and do not hinder them, for the kingdom of God belongs to such as these. I tell you the truth, anyone who will not receive the kingdom of God like a little child will never enter it." And he took the children in his arms, put his hands on them and blessed them (Mark 10:13-16).

Because of this innate childlike ability, early childhood is a unique opportunity to help our children build strong faith. I would argue that some of the most effective Christians are those who accepted the Kingdom and all of its consequences as a child and then were discipled and nurtured by parents into a sustainable and mature faith. I talk about this process in my first book, *Give Your Kids the Keys.*

The Testing of Our Faith

One of the discipling challenges parents face happens when their children begin to reach an age of understanding and reason. It is at this pivotal point that children come to realize that everything they believe for does not automatically come to fruition. When this happens, many kids, and adults, stagger in their belief.

The first thing we need to understand is that every time our kids are presented with an obstacle to faith, they are also afforded the opportunity to create a more sustainable faith. After all, it is in the testing of our faith that we learn to persevere. If you try to remove all doubt from your kids, all extended struggles of belief, you will actually be destabilizing their walk of faith.

> Because you know that the testing of your faith develops perseverance (Jas. 1:3).

One of the reasons people lose faith in times of testing is that they have put their hope in the gift rather than the Giver. We are never called to believe in the result of any prayer, but rather in the One who bestows prayerful results. This means that when we believe for a mountain to be moved, we are actually believing in the One who can move the mountain instead of concentrating on or trying to muster up enough perceived faith to cause that mountain to move. The latter type of faith is more about mental concentration then Kingdom-bringing trust.

When raising your kids to have great faith, you will want to make sure that you disciple them to take no stock in how things might play out on the ground. Results are up to God. Kingdom-bringing faith always looks to the miracle worker and accepts the results with a Romans 8:28 outlook:

> And we know that in all things God works for the good of those who love him, who have been called according to his purpose (Rom. 8:28).

Believing kids who have the gift of faith have a greater ability to believe for what they cannot see, or for an earthly impossibility, than other believers. These Christian kids hold loosely to the results their eyes see and look toward heaven with hope.

Your kid might have the gift of faith if you see this pattern:

- He/she makes statements of belief in God's ability.
- Prays for and believes in miracles.
- Displays hope when others doubt.

- Tends to be more optimistic about life.
- Believes the Word of God at face value.
- Often speaks hope to others.
- Has courage in difficult situations or tends to walk in boldness.
- Is willing to take on large and difficult projects that might cause others to hesitate.
- Is incredibly trusting.

Miracles

The spiritual gift of *miracles* is the ability to partner with God to see supernatural power influence the natural order of things. Miracles are a part of being a Christian. When God influences the natural order of things to manifest His will, we have experienced a miracle. The ability to partner with God in these events became available to all believers upon the Holy Spirit's impartation at Pentecost (see Acts 2).

> I tell you the truth, anyone who has faith in me will do what I have been doing. He will do even greater things than these, because I am going to the Father (John 14:12).

Miracles happen for all sorts of reasons. Jesus used miracles as an evangelistic witness to His power. These works of power were meant to encourage salvific faith. Christ also used miracles to bring mercy and comfort to the hurting. Mercy and comfort are two of the primary reasons for the use of miracles in our modern context.

- *Miracles for salvation*: "But if I do it, even though you do not believe me, believe the miracles, that you may know and understand that the Father is in me, and I in the Father" (John 10:38). "Believe me when I say that I am in the Father and the Father is in me; or at least believe on the evidence of the miracles themselves" (John 14:11).

- *Miracles and compassion*: "When Jesus landed and saw a large crowd, he had compassion on them and healed their sick" (Matt. 14:14). "Jesus had compassion on them and touched their eyes. Immediately they received their sight and followed him" (Matt. 20:34).

Believers who have the gift of miracles are not miracle workers, but rather conduits of God's power. While all believers have miracle-working power at their disposal, if God so desires, Christians with the gift of miracles are those whom God has chosen to work through in this way more often than He does in others.

One thing we must understand about the gift of miracles is that it is more about a believer's availability to God's timing and will than possessing some type of supernatural power of his or her own. Unlike superman or superwoman, miracle workers are just normal believers that God has decided to use as a tool for implementing His works of power, evangelism and compassion in ways that go beyond the ordinary. We see this principle in the life of the apostle Paul:

God did extraordinary miracles through Paul (Acts 19:11).

Miracles happened "through" Paul, not because of Paul. The more we step out in faith and ask God to go beyond what we define as the normal order of things, the more opportunity we allow for miracles to happen and the more opportunity we have to be conduits of His power.

In the Scripture, we see four primary types of miracles:

1. Miracles over nature:

   - "During the fourth watch of the night Jesus went out to them, walking on the lake" (Matt. 14:25).

   - "The disciples went and woke him, saying, 'Master, Master, we're going to drown!' He got up and rebuked the wind and the raging waters; the storm subsided, and all was calm" (Luke 8:24).

2. Miracles of provision:

- "But so that we may not offend them, go to the lake and throw out your line. Take the first fish you catch; open its mouth and you will find a four-drachma coin. Take it and give it to them for my tax and yours" (Matt. 17:27).

- "Jesus said, 'Have the people sit down.' There was plenty of grass in that place, and the men sat down, about five thousand of them. Jesus then took the loaves, gave thanks, and distributed to those who were seated as much as they wanted. He did the same with the fish. When they had all had enough to eat, he said to his disciples, 'Gather the pieces that are left over. Let nothing be wasted.' So they gathered them and filled twelve baskets with the pieces of the five barley loaves left over by those who had eaten. After the people saw the miraculous sign that Jesus did, they began to say, 'Surely this is the Prophet who is to come into the world'" (John 6:10-14).

3. Miracles of healing:

- "His father was sick in bed, suffering from fever and dysentery. Paul went in to see him and, after prayer, placed his hands on him and healed him" (Acts 28:8).

- "But Jesus answered, 'No more of this!' And he touched the man's ear and healed him" (Luke 22:51).

4. Miracles over demonic strongholds (this is listed as an evangelistic gift, as it releases people from bondage that would otherwise inhibit salvation):

- "Crowds gathered also from the towns around Jerusalem, bringing their sick and those tormented by evil spirits, and all of them were healed" (Acts 5:16).

- "With shrieks, evil spirits came out of many, and many paralytics and cripples were healed" (Acts 8:7).

In twenty-plus years of ministry, I have personally seen all four types of these miracles. While hiking in the hills above Hong Kong with a group of high school students, a girl on our trip was stung by a wasp. Since she was allergic to bee stings, she immediately went into shock, and a large bump appeared on her arm. She was sweating profusely and her breathing was getting more and more shallow.

We were miles from help; all we could do was pray. We gathered around her, laid hands on her and began to ask God to heal her. Right away the sweats and shallow breathing ceased and she began to stabilize. Still, there was still that nasty welt on her arm. Encouraged, we prayed again, this time specifically for the large bump on her forearm. As we prayed, it vanished. When we removed our hands from her arm, there was only a pinprick left. She was healed! We kept on hiking.

While this particular instance might also be listed under the gift of healing category, it was just one of many miracles we experienced on that trip. One other dramatic event happened when one of our team members was preaching to a group of people who were being inhibited from hearing the teaching because of a blistering rain that was hitting hard on the tin roof above us. It was the kind of pounding rain that I have only experienced in the tropics.

As he preached, the speaker felt God speak to his heart and encourage him to command the rain to stop. Oddly, this thought came with a type of holy anger due to the fact that the Word of God was being inhibited. Out of nowhere, he yelled out, "Rain, be ceased, in the name of Jesus!" Bam! Just like that, the rain stopped. And I don't mean trickled off slowly, I mean stopped. To this day, I have never seen so much rain stop immediately. It was as if a sharp knife had cut the rain off and it fell to the ground in the same way a pail of water would if you were to dump it from the sky.

The people who were sitting close enough to hear him command the rain to cease were shocked. I was shocked. Amazed himself, he said, "Did you see that?" He was as dumbfounded as the rest of us. The cool part of the story is that the sun came out and the preaching and teaching of the Word of God went out to people who needed to hear it. It was an amazing experience!

Your kid might have the gift of miracles if you have witnessed the following pattern:

- He/she has prayed for, believed for and perhaps experienced God's provision.
- Has prayed for and seen someone healed.
- Prays with effectiveness over places or people mired in spiritual darkness.
- Has prayed and believed for a miracle over nature.

Tongues as an Evangelistic Gift

The spiritual gift of *tongues* is given to believers for the purpose of communicating the gospel to people of a different language. In the book of Acts, we see that the gospel was spread through the use of tongues. In Acts 2, when the Holy Spirit descended on God's people, they began to speak in foreign tongues. Visitors from other countries who had come to Jerusalem for the festival understood these tongues.

Now there were staying in Jerusalem God-fearing Jews from every nation under heaven. When they heard this sound, a crowd came together in bewilderment, because each one heard them speaking in his own language. Utterly amazed, they asked: "Are not all these men who are speaking Galileans? Then how is it that each of us hears them in his own native language? Parthians, Medes and Elamites; residents of Mesopotamia, Judea and Cappadocia, Pontus and Asia, Phrygia and Pamphylia, Egypt and the parts of Libya near Cyrene; visitors from Rome (both

Jews and converts to Judaism); Cretans and Arabs—we hear them declaring the wonders of God in our own tongues!" (Acts 2:5-11).

I have heard of many missionaries who have experienced this when going into other cultures. One of the most dramatic stories was a missionary to New Guinea who was able to immediately communicate in the language of the tribal people upon arriving to their village for the first time.

Your kids might have the gift of tongues if you notice this pattern:

- He/she speaks in tongues.
- A person has been saved because of his/her use of tongues.
- He/she has acquired a language while ministering to a foreign people group.

Missions

The spiritual gift of *missions* is the God-given desire and ability to minister effectively in a foreign culture or subculture.

In 2004, Karie, Lily and I sold our home, packed up everything and headed for Australia with the intent of living and ministering there for the unforeseen future. After a year of amazing ministry, and with our marriage in a rough spot, we decided it was time to return home. For us, family comes after God, but before ministry.

Before we left America to go to Australia, we began to be overwhelmed with a burden for Australia and its people. It was a burden that even superseded our call to ministry in California. The more we prayed and moved in faith toward our goal of living in Australia, the greater our desire grew to see that nation experience revival. Living in America was getting extremely difficult as this burden increased.

While we might end up back in Australia someday, we currently don't feel the same burden we experienced in 2004. Today,

I am still processing the missionary calling in our life. Do Karie and I have the spiritual gift of missions, or was this just a season in our life and ministry career? I am still unsure.

Lifelong missionaries are an amazing breed. These are believers who feel more comfortable in a culture that is not their own. They have such a burden for another culture and its people that it propels them in faith to overcome the difficulties and challenges they will experience on the field.

A Three-Year-Old Missionary?

Karie and I are currently in a season of testing the missionary gift in our three-year-old Lucy's life. This is because we have sensed that God might have a future in missions for her.

As we have prayerfully tested this possible calling, God has made us aware of many possible clues. Here are a few that might give you an understanding of how we process giftings within our kids.

Lucy is a wanderer. If you don't keep an eye on Lucy, she will bolt. She does not do this to be disobedient; she just likes to explore and is not afraid to get lost. I know this sounds like a strange way to see a missionary gift in my daughter, but is this not what missionaries do? Missionaries are not afraid to wander off. Lucy is not a child who is driven by fear. Remember, even the things our kids do that we don't appreciate, like wandering off unattended, can point to some deeper work of God.

Lucy is really good at picking up languages. She just seems to have the ability to quickly assimilate new words into her vocabulary. We regularly hear her counting to 10 in Spanish after watching the latest episode of *Dora the Explorer*.

The last characteristic we have noticed about Lucy in regard to missions is that she is easily adaptable. Lucy is not fussy, and she goes with the flow. This is a quality that many missionaries need. On the mission field, especially during the pioneering of a new work, things change rapidly and missionaries need to be able to adjust on the fly, to adapt. This is something that comes naturally to Lucy.

As I said earlier, we have begun to test this possible gifting in Lucy. I use the word "test" because we don't want to anoint or put expectations on either of our children. Rather than tell Lucy that she is a missionary, we are implementing a plan to test this in her.

South American Missionary Gift Testing

Thanks to the generous support of some amazing friends and supporters, my family and I just returned from a 10-day trip to YWAM's (Youth With A Mission) base in Pichilemu, Chile. This was our first international missions trip as a family since Lucy was born. We hope to go on many more.

While there were a lot of reasons for this trip, part of Karie's and my plan was to get Lucy on the mission field to see what God might do in her heart. As expected, Lucy did amazingly well. She traveled the 25-hour journey by plane and cramped bus like a champion. She never complained. In the 10 days we were there, Lucy's understanding and comprehension of Spanish went through the roof.

Just yesterday, Lucy told me that one day when she grows up, she wants to live in Chile. While I am not sure this means that Lucy has a missionary gifting, I can assure you that we are going to keep testing!

Test everything. Hold on to the good (1 Thess. 5:21).

Your kid might have the gift of missions if you notice the following pattern:

- He/she is interested in travel.
- Tends to be interested in foreign cultures and people.
- Is good at language assimilation.
- Wanders off without fear.
- Exhibits great faith.
- Shares the gospel.
- Is content with less stuff than other kids.

PART THREE

Releasing Kids into Their Gifts

My sister, Lucy's, spiritual gifts are knowledge, giving, wisdom, missionary and interpretation of tongues. When my dad reads the Bible, Lucy is knowledgeable because she asks such great questions about the story. Sometimes she sounds like an adult. She is giving, because if you ask to play with her dolly, I bet she would say yes.

I think wisdom is a hard one to explain, so I am skipping to the next definition. She is a little missionary because for two weeks in Chile, she was really good at helping at the missionary base.

Once my dad spoke in a tongue and Lucy interpreted it. Two other adults said that they got the same interpretation after Lucy spoke up.

My spiritual gifts are leadership, tongues, missionary and giving. I am not going to define them though. Enjoy the rest of the book.

Lily, Age 9
Our Daughter

Seeds and Fruit

Hearing and Seeing God's Gifts in Your Kids

Size matters not. Look at me. Judge me by my size, do you? Hmm?
Hmm. And well you should not. For my ally is the Force, and a powerful
ally it is. Luminous beings are we, not this crude matter.

YODA

Now that you have a good idea of what spiritual gifts in your kids look like, you will want to begin to inquire of the Lord as you put into practice what you have discovered. This will be of utmost importance as you begin to clearly identify spiritual gifts and callings for your children.

God Is in the Communication Business

Over and over again within the story of God's Word, we see that God speaks to parents about their children. God is still in that business. If we listen to and seek God for our children's life purpose and direction, especially in the area of spiritual gifts, God will make them known to us. This has been the case with both of our girls. Here are a few biblical examples of parents to whom God spoke about their offspring:

- **Abraham:** "Then the word of the LORD came to him: 'This man will not be your heir, but a son coming from your own body will be your heir.' He took him outside and said, 'Look up at the heavens and count the stars—if indeed you can count them.' Then he said to him, 'So shall your off-spring be.' Abram believed the LORD, and he credited it to him as righteousness" (Gen. 15:4-6).

- **Isaac and Rebekah:** "Isaac prayed to the LORD on behalf of his wife, because she was barren. The LORD answered his prayer, and his wife Rebekah became pregnant. The babies jostled each other within her, and she said, 'Why is this happening to me?' So she went to inquire of the LORD. The LORD said to her, 'Two nations are in your womb, and two peoples from within you will be separated; one people will be stronger than the other, and the older will serve the younger'" (Gen. 25:21-23).

- **Zechariah:** Then an angel of the Lord appeared to him, standing at the right side of the altar of incense. When Zechariah saw him, he was startled and was gripped with fear. But the angel said to him: 'Do not be afraid, Zechariah; your prayer has been heard. Your wife Elizabeth will bear you a son, and you are to give him the name John. He will be a joy and delight to you, and many will rejoice because of his birth, for he will be great in the sight of the Lord. He is never to take wine or other fermented drink, and he will be filled with the Holy Spirit even from birth. Many of the people of Israel will he bring back to the Lord their God. And he will go on before the Lord, in the spirit and power of Elijah, to turn the hearts of the fathers to their children and the disobedient to the wisdom of the righteous—to make ready a people prepared for the Lord'" (Luke 1:11-17).

- **Mary:** "But the angel said to her, 'Do not be afraid, Mary, you have found favor with God. You will be with child and give birth to a son, and you are to give him the name Jesus. He will be great and will be called the Son of the Most High. The Lord God will give him the throne of his father David, and he will reign over the house of Jacob forever; his kingdom will never end'" (Luke 1:30-33).

- **Joseph and Mary:** "Now there was a man in Jerusalem called Simeon, who was righteous and devout. He was waiting for the consolation of Israel, and the Holy Spirit was upon him. It had been revealed to him by the Holy Spirit that he would not die before he had seen the Lord Christ. Moved by the Spirit, he went into the temple courts. When the parents brought in the child Jesus to do for him what the custom of the Law required, Simeon took him in his arms and praised God, saying: 'Sovereign LORD, as you have promised, you now dismiss your servant in peace. For my eyes have seen your salvation, which you have prepared in the sight of all people, a light for revelation to the Gentiles and for glory to your people Israel.' The child's father and mother marveled at what was said about him. Then Simeon blessed them and said to Mary, his mother: 'This child is destined to cause the falling and rising of many in Israel, and to be a sign that will be spoken against, so that the thoughts of many hearts will be revealed. And a sword will pierce your own soul too.' There was also a prophetess, Anna, the daughter of Phanuel, of the tribe of Asher. She was very old; she had lived with her husband seven years after her marriage, and then was a widow until she was eighty-four. She never left the temple but worshiped night and day, fasting and praying. Coming up to them at that very moment, she gave thanks to God and spoke about the child to all who were looking forward to the redemption of Jerusalem" (Luke 2:25-38).

In these Scripture passages we see a few elements at play as these parents heard from God about their kids. The first element is that

God spoke on His own volition. He is God, after all. When God wants you to know something about your kids, He is going to tell you. Next, we see parents who inquired of the LORD in regard to their children. When Rebekah sensed a struggle within her womb, she "inquired of the LORD."

Finally, we see that the body of believers was an active part of discerning a child's gifting. This is important. Before we had spiritual gifts tests, we had each other. One of the greatest proofs of your giftings is when other Spirit-led believers recognize your gifts in you.

> Before we had spiritual gifts tests, we had each other. One of the greatest proofs of your giftings is when other Spirit-led believers recognize your gifts in you.

Because of this, you might want to have a few other family members or close friends take the spiritual gifts survey located in the back of this book. I would suggest seeking as many qualified opinions as possible. God's voice is often confirmed in unity.

Isaac prayed to the LORD on behalf of his wife, because she was barren. The LORD answered his prayer, and his wife Rebekah became pregnant. The babies jostled each other within her, and she said, "Why is this happening to me?" So she went to inquire of the LORD (Gen. 25:21-22).

Ask God for Insight into Your Kids

People inquire of God when they believe He will answer them. We are not responsible for the answering; that is God's job. What we are responsible for as mothers and fathers is to inquire of the Lord for our children. Whether they are in a difficult season or coasting along smoothly, we want to inquire of the Lord for our children. As we seek God for understanding of our children's spiritual gifts, it will be important to regularly go before God in prayer and ask for understanding and guidance.

Many believers do not inquire of the Lord, because they don't know how to identify when God speaks to them. They are prone to deny what they have heard. I'm not saying they do this on purpose, but for some reason, the majority of believers I meet more often think that something is not really from God as opposed to the other way around. Thoughts like, *How do I know this was not just my mind?* are some of the biggest silencers of God's voice. The Bible assures us that God communicates with His children. God speaks all the time, in very clear ways, but we doubt that it is God.

When was the last time you heard from God? What did you do when you became aware of something that might have been from God? Did you move too fast before testing that word, or did you minimize and disregard it? One of the marks of a mature believer is to live in the balance of these responses.

If a word or insight is truly from God, you rarely need to tell the person you are giving the word to that it was from God. This is because God's words bear fruit. If a word is from God, it will hit its mark. Instead of always telling my kids that God said something to me, I will just share what I think I heard from God. Other times, I will say something like, "This is what I think I heard from God. What do you guys think?" In this way, I try to faithfully test what I believe God has shared with me.

Seeds and Fruit

Insights and words from God are like seeds. Whenever you think you hear from God, take that word and plant it, because true words from God always grow and bear fruit. Once that word is planted, you will begin the watering and fertilizing process. We do this through prayer, observation, stepping out in faith, checking the fruit and beginning the process again.

It's like the apple tree at Karie's parents' cabin. Every fall, this tree produces enough apples to easily make 500 apple pies. I am not kidding. I had no idea how productive apple trees can be.

Right before the first freeze, the apples are most ripe. Hundreds of apples are weighing down the branches and still hundreds more are at the base of the tree, having fallen from the boughs. It is nearly impossible to walk within 25 feet of that tree without making applesauce. Apples are everywhere.

Words and insights from God are the same way. If you test them with wisdom and discernment, there is no way they will not produce abundant fruit. This is how you help your children discern their giftings. Just look for the fruit. If there is no fruit, what you are seeing is probably not a special gift from God. If your kid has a spiritual gift in one area or another, the evidence of God working through them will be all over it. In the next chapter, we will look at how you can provide a platform for your kids to test out the possible gifts you have identified in them through this process of seeking.

Our good friends Dave and Kate are Spirit-led parents who have been employing this process with their kids. Below is a recent email I received from them. It discusses their journey with their children and their desire to not project gifts on their kids, but rather follow God in His promptings.

> Hi Adam,
>
> I think for us, we've noticed our kids having certain tendencies toward spiritual gifts, and we point them out to the kids so they can enjoy knowing they are gifted in certain ways. It's great that they identify themselves as having God-given strengths. But on the other hand, we are hesitant to typecast them at a young age. For example, from the age of four or five, Anna has been the first one to encourage us to pray about a situation, usually before I even think to. She'll pipe up, "You should pray about that!" even though Dave and I aren't overly vocal about prayer. We model it and talk about it, but not like one of those couples who are constantly stopping to pray about everything. Anna just innately seems to want to turn to prayer first thing. So we started praising her as "our little

prayer warrior." I don't think anything is wrong with that, and she was clearly delighted that we were delighted with her. But I felt Maddie in the background, subconsciously categorizing herself: Anna is the prayer warrior; I am not a prayer warrior (because Mom and Dad don't affirm that in me). Plus, I don't want Anna growing up thinking, *I pray, Maddie serves . . . that's the way it always will be.* I want her to look beyond the one obvious strength/gift she has to others as well.

I guess I'll be interested to see how you address the fact that we want to affirm our kids without typecasting them. Not sure if that is helpful or not!

Here is my response to Dave and Kate:

You bring up a great point, and one that I am going to stress in the book. How do we edify our kids while not typecasting them? The key to that is fruit. The proof is in the pudding. If your child has a real spiritual gift, you will know it, and they will know it. It will keep coming out. Through discernment and constant visible proof, you will eventually want to make sure that you solidify them in these giftings. While the fear of not projecting on our kids is a real concern, Christians are called to identify gifts in each other and implement those gifts. This is what Paul did with young Timothy. Just the fact that you have this concern shows me that you are most likely not going to jam "gifts teaching" down their throats.

With our kids, we say, "Hey, Mom and I think you might have this or that gift from God. How about we test it out." In this way, we let our kids lead the way, but we are making sure that we host fruit-picking opportunities along the way. This is the job of a parent in this arena. Identify and allow opportunity. First Thessalonians 5:20-21 says that we are to test everything. After we pick the fruit, we test it. We talk about the experience. If it was a good test, we keep doing it.

One thing I would shy away from is using terms like "little prayer warrior." I think comments like this, while encouraging, can lead to pride and/or jealousy from siblings. It sets the bar too high. I would instead just be matter of fact. Say something like, "Hey, Anna, it seems that God might have given you a gift of intercession/prayer. That is so cool. How do you think we can use that?"

One battle we face is helping our children not compete. It seems that every time I tell Lucy I love her, or I encourage her in some way, Lily has to say, "What about me?" While the desire is to immediately comfort the asking child with, "Well, I love you too" or "You are also a great encourager," I try to stay away from this. I want my kids to be comfortable in their own skin. What I usually do is pull them aside later and say, "Hey, this is who your sister is." Then I tell the asking child who she is, as I know her to be. I want both of my girls to be completely separate in regard to their unique identities.

One thing I did tell Lily last night after she challenged me in my love for her, after I had told Lucy how special she was to me, was, "I want you to know that I could never love you any more than I do. You already have my whole heart." She liked that answer.

Thanks Dave and Kate, hope that helps.

Building a Vehicle
They Can Drive

Give Your Kids the Keys to Their Gifts

Not long ago, I was watching one of the extreme video shows that air on Saturday afternoons. About halfway through the show the announcer warned us to turn away if we were squeamish. Unfortunately, that pronouncement usually has the opposite effect on me. I tuned in. The video showed a four-year-old child whose parents had given him a motorcycle for his birthday. The results were disastrous. Unable to use the brake properly, the boy drove straight into the open tailgate of a truck, taking the full brunt of the impact to his forehead. Thankfully, the boy survived a cracked skull and made a full recovery.

This story represents what we don't want to do when releasing our children into their gifts. Instead, we need to test our kid's gifts by building vehicles they can drive, vehicles that fit their life stage and abilities. We do this because of the nature of spiritual gifts. Spiritual gifts are not proven by the taking of a test, but rather in the testing of faith. The task now at hand is to expose your children to opportunities and environments where their perceived gifts can be proven—places where your kids can succeed and be edified in their faith.

As I stated a few chapters back, you already know how to do this. Most of you have begun the process of introducing and incorporating things like sports, the arts and academics into your kids' lives. The manner in which you undertake this challenge will, in large part, determine whether your son or daughter embraces his or her gifts and individual call to ministry. But don't let that stress you out; God will lead you in this. The key is that you are now engaged in releasing your kids into ministry.

> Spiritual gifts are not proven by the taking of
> a test, but rather in the testing of faith.

I am sure you have all seen the gifted athlete who walks away from sports because of his or her parents' driving and overbearing natures. The other extreme, and equally faith-killing, are the parents who never challenge their children beyond their own appetites and desires. When we exchange comfort for growth, our faith dies a slow and painful death.[1]

At the sake of being redundant, let me affirm that you already know how to do this. Let's look at sports for a minute. If you are a sports parent, I am pretty sure you did not let your five-year-old try out for the varsity team. No, you started in the backyard when he or she was still in diapers. You were consistent and tireless in your pursuit. You bought a ball that fit your child's hand instead of the one the professionals use. You did this because you knew your kid would quickly lose interest if he or she never succeeded in throwing and catching the ball a few times.

Each time your child caught the ball, he or she beamed. With each catch, you encouraged your child. You heaped on the praise, and your child responded. Some of you quickly realized your kid was a natural, and dreams of a professional career spun in your mind. Others of you could not stand seeing the ball bounce off your child's face one more time, and you decided that you should begin testing for other traits and aptitudes.

Now you are going to do the same thing as you test your child's spiritual gifts. The difference is that this time, instead of getting your child behind the wheel of his or her natural abilities, which will eventually fade as they age, you are going to give your kids the keys to a Kingdom that never fades, but rather increases in momentum each time your child steps out in faith.

> I will give you the keys of the kingdom of heaven; whatever you bind on earth will be bound in heaven, and whatever you loose on earth will be loosed in heaven (Matt. 16:19).

Vehicles that Kids Can Drive

Here are a few ideas your kids can test-drive to kick the tires of their spiritual gifts. I pray you have the time of your life while riding shotgun!

Prophecy

- Study the Old Testament prophets and prophecy. I was able to find a lot of great-looking resources on Amazon by searching the following: "prophets kids Christian." This search should yield lots of age-appropriate material to get you started.
- Ask your kids to pray about your family's future and ask them to tell you if God clearly reveals anything to them.
- Host listening times where your kids take a few minutes to tune in to God's silence. Ask them what they might have sensed from the Holy Spirit.
- Memorize Scripture together. God often leads our future through scriptural insight.

Teaching

- Ask your church's children's pastor or coordinator if your kid can teach a lower-grade-level Bible lesson at church.
- Let your kid lead family devotions.
- Study Scripture with your child.
- Start a discipleship program at your church, where older kids spend time discipling younger children.
- Volunteer with your kid at the local library, teaching other kids to read.

Miracles

- Study the topic of miracles with your child. I was able to find a lot of interesting resources on the topic of miracles by searching the following combined words on Amazon: "miracles kids Christians." The search yielded everything from classic missionary stories to cartoons.
- Pray for miracles of healing, provision, protection, and so on. Miracles often happen because of prayer. Keep a journal with your child to record your prayers and their results.
- Visit missionaries in the Third World. I'm not sure why, but most of the miracles I have seen have been in the Third World. Perhaps their lack of material possessions and the distractions we live with on a daily basis prepare their hearts for greater faith and focus on what is truly important. More likely it is because these cultures have been less influenced by secular modernism.

Healing

- Take your children to visit and pray for the sick.
- Volunteer at a local children's hospital.
- Create a visual tool your family can use to pray for the sick. Perhaps make a collage of faces your kids can view, or a photo album, or pictures pasted to three-by-five-inch cards with a whole punched in the corner and held together with a ring . . . Make it simple, and let your children have a hand in creating the visual tool and choosing people you will pray for each day.
- Work to develop compassion in your child. One way to do this is by exposing him or her to the less fortunate. Work at a homeless shelter or create a family ministry project. The holidays are a rich time of need to do this. Compassion is often the fuel of healing.

Administration

- Let your child administrate part of your family ministry project. After you and your family have picked a project, allow your child to organize the details.

- Volunteer for an administrative project at a community or church event.

Tongues and Interpretation of Tongues
- Study this gift with your kids. This can be done by referencing the Scriptures presented in chapter 3 or by searching the Internet for articles on this gifting.
- Let your kids hear you speak in tongues, and ask if God gave them an interpretation.
- Pray and ask God for this gift, if it be His will.

Wisdom
- Bring your kids into the family decision-making process.
- Challenge your kids to seek God for answers to their problems rather than answering every question for them.
- Value your children's wise input and encourage more.
- Ask them what they would do in a given situation.
- Read from the book of Proverbs every day. You could make a proverb a day part of your family's mealtime talk.

Knowledge
- Study Scripture with your children and ask them what insights come to mind.
- Let your kids lead a Bible study.
- After a prayer time, ask your kids if they have anything to offer that God might have put on their hearts.

Faith
- Don't fix everything for your kids. Let them exhibit faith and trust in God for the results.
- Let them participate in a ministry bigger than themselves.
- Start a ministry with your kids that you could not accomplish unless God shows up.
- Sign up for a missions trip you can't afford. (Could be a monumental faith builder!)
- Pray for the sick.

- The gift of faith is a rich category in which to use a journal to record your and your children's walk of faith.

Discernment

- Ask your kids to chime in on spiritual matters. What do they think God is saying?
- Encourage your kids to express when they are sensing God's presence or leading.
- Ask your children what they think God's opinion is of certain advertisements they might see, and why.

Evangelist

- Challenge your kids to invite their friends to church.
- Go on an outreach as a family ministry.
- Teach your kids how to clearly share the gospel with their friends.
- Pray for the lost as a family.

Pastors

- Teach your kids what a pastor does.
- If possible, spend an afternoon hanging with your pastor at work.
- Challenge your child to pastorally care for his or her sports team or drama club.
- Train your child to disciple a younger sibling.
- Challenge your children to care for the outcast.

Service

- Volunteer as a family at a local service project.
- Ask your children to come up with a potential list of ways to help others.
- Go on a local missions project together.

Encouragement

- Train your children to write notes of encouragement to others.

- Challenge your children to dream up ways to encourage others in their pursuits.
- Let your children host a celebration for another person.

Giving

- Teach your kids to tithe.
- Support a kid through one of the major sponsorship non-profit organizations.
- Provide your child with opportunities to give.
- Find as many ways as possible to make your child aware of the needs of others.

Leadership

- Encourage your child to run for a student government position.
- Plan an event and let your child take the lead.
- Help your child lead a Bible study.
- Let your child be a camp counselor for younger kids.

Mercy

- Minister with your children at a local hospital or shelter for the less fortunate.
- Expose your children to age-appropriate dilemmas (poverty, hunger, disease, and so forth).
- Teach your children to share their abundance of material things with, and pray for, others in need.

Missions

- Study the biographies of famous missionaries and read them aloud as a family. These faith-filled stories make for great bedtime reading. One of the best websites I have found is http://www.fish4him.org/FamousMissionaries/tabid/141/language/en-US/Default.aspx. Here you can find a list of every missionary from the Salvation Army's William Booth to Eric Liddell of *Chariots of Fire* fame.
- Go on a missions trip together.

Intercession/Prayer

- Pray daily with your kids.
- Let them lead prayer times.
- Prayer-walk their school campus.
- Create a prayer book or screen saver program that represents the people you pray for.
- Let your children write out prayers to God in the family prayer journal. Be sure to record God's answers!

Hospitality

- Let your children usher at church.
- Let your children help in the planning of an upcoming party or event.
- Help your children host a party.
- Encourage your children to volunteer at a home for the elderly.

Helps

- Suggest ways that your child could lend a hand to a friend.
- Volunteer with your children at a community meal or soup kitchen, or . . .
- Be aware as a family of people in need and be willing to stop what you are doing to help out.

May God bless you as you give your kids the keys (Matt. 16:19)!
—Adam, Karie, Lily and Lucy Stadtmiller

Note

1. This is a direct quote from a sermon by Steve Forsyth, the pastor of El Cajon Wesleyan church.

Spiritual Gifts Test

What's Your Kid's Ministry?

In your hands you have an incredible resource that, if used under the guidance of the Holy Spirit, will not only give you a deeper insight into your children but also help you guide and direct them into their personal ministry. The following is intended to aid you in making the *Discover Your Kid's Spiritual Gifts* assessment an easy and understandable tool to use.

Why a Spiritual Gifts Test?

Now concerning spiritual gifts, *brethren,*
I do not want you to be unaware.

1 CORINTHIANS 12:1, NASB,
EMPHASIS ADDED

Spiritual gifts are not "magic" but are tools given to us by God and through the Holy Spirit that allow us to be more effective in Christ and in ministry. These spiritual abilities are to be stewarded. Every believer is called to know and walk in the gift or gifts he or she has been given. This is as true for adults as it is for kids. The Discover Your Kid's Spiritual Gifts test and assessment was created for the purpose of helping believers identify their Kids' unique giftings and where they fit in God's divine purpose more effectively.

Taking the Test

The *Discover Your Kid's Spiritual Gifts* assessment tool is unlike other tests in that the child being tested is not the individual responding to the questions. Rather, you as a parent are assessing what you know to be true about your son or daughter. This type of testing allows for a more efficient way of assessing a wide age range of children and allows more than one person involved in the child's life to take the test. You might want to invite parents, grandparents, close friends and perhaps even your child's Sunday School teacher to take the test. This multiple testing model will help create a less biased result.

There are 80 questions in the assessment. For each question, rate the child on a scale of 1 to 5, as follows:

1=Never
2=Rarely
3=Occasionally
4=Often
5=Always

There are four questions in the assessment for each gift, which appear in random order. Once you have answered each question, use the assessment key on page 152 to determine you child's particular spiritual giftings.

Helpful Hints

- Take the test before and after you read this book. Taking the test before you read the book will provide you with questions that the book will answer. The post-test results will provide a more accurate and informed assessment.
- Spend a few minutes in prayer before taking the test. Settle your mind and ask the Holy Spirit to lead you.
- Don't worry about perfect answers. You will be testing these results on the playing field of real ministry.

• If multiple people take the test for your child, combine all of the totals. This will allow you to get a collective view of what your child's gifts are.

What If I Make a Mistake in Assessing My Child?

The spiritual gifts test and assessment is meant to act as more of a compass then a map. While this test can be incredibly effective at highlighting potential giftings, the gifts identified must still be tried and tested. If you have answered for your child in a way that provides a false positive, it will prove out in the testing of that gift. This will happen as you minister and explore different ministry opportunities alongside your child.

How Will I Know If These Results Are Correct?

True giftings will produce fruit. Your job as a parent is to provide a platform for your child to explore the findings this test produces. For example, if your child is shown to have a gift of teaching, that gift must be put into action and shown to bear fruit on a consistent basis before you could assume that gifting truly exists. With that said, there is no harm in implementing a fertile proving ground for your child to explore different gifts and ministries in Christ. Test your results!

A Word of Wisdom

The *Discover Your Kid's Spiritual Gifts* assessment is to be used in conjunction with the source material in this book. While taking the assessment will provide you with a valuable result whether you have read the book or not, the results will be much more accurate once you understand how each gifting might be displayed in your child and/or children in general.

Enjoy your adventure in Christ!
Pastor Adam Stadtmiller

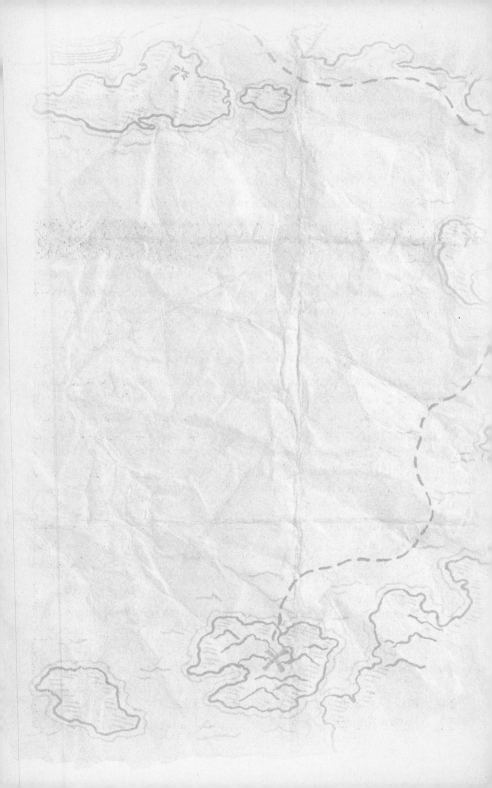

Gifts Assessment

For each question, indicate to what extent it is true of your child using the following scale:

1=Never **2**=Rarely **3**=Occasionally **4**=Often **5**=Always

	Question	Response 1-5
1	I have caught my child praying on his or her own initiative and without prompting.	
2	My child is not overly protective of his or her things.	
3	My child would include kids who are shunned by other kids in games or sporting events.	
4	My son or daughter is less critical or negative than other children.	
5	My son or daughter is a visionary—he or she can see and communicate what others don't see.	
6	My child enjoys being organized.	
7	My child is a good judge of character. He or she shies away from some but goes to others.	
8	On a family trip to the zoo, my child would be the one most verbal about what he or she wants everyone to go and see.	
9	My child enjoys helping other people.	
10	My child is often content with what he or she has.	
11	My child shares the gospel in a way appropriate to his or her age.	
12	My son or daughter has voiced God's plans for our family before they have happened.	
13	There is a noticeable, enjoyable change in my son or daughter's demeanor when he or she is in the midst of helping others.	
14	My child might cry or express emotion when others are expressing their pain in words or in tears.	

	Question	Response 1-5
15	My child displays courage with a belief in God's protection and provision.	
16	My son or daughter believes the Word of God at face value.	
17	My son or daughter communicates verbally or with the written word with great clarity.	
18	My son or daughter likes to meet new people and help them feel welcomed and accepted.	
19	My son or daughter regularly encourages others.	
20	My child makes faith-filled statements about God's healing ability or exhibits faith in God's ability to heal.	
21	My child offers to pray for others without prompting.	
22	My son or daughter is extremely friendly.	
23	My son or daughter has spoken words of God's knowledge that have proven to be true.	
24	My son or daughter is good at teaching and explaining things to others.	
25	My son or daughter is nurturing and empathetic.	
26	My son or daughter makes faith-filled statements of belief in God's ability.	
27	My child gives others second chances and forgives more easily then others.	
28	My child has stated that God has spoken to him or her about a future event.	
29	My son or daughter makes wise decisions.	
30	When working to complete a task for another person, my son or daughter is focused and cheerful.	
31	My child is unafraid to speak with others about Jesus.	
32	My son or daughter is sensitive to things that are spiritually dark (e.g., books, movies, places).	
33	My son or daughter tends to see the best in others.	
34	My son or daughter volunteers quickly, even when the task at hand might be difficult.	

1=Never   2= Rarely   3=Occasionally   4=Often   5=Always

	Question	Response 1-5
35	My child is aware of time, and timeliness is important to him or her.	
36	My son or daughter invites friends to church.	
37	My child tends to use stories, word pictures and analogies when describing things.	
38	My son or daughter is conscience of things that are fair and unfair.	
39	My child has had dreams, thoughts or visions about future events.	
40	My child is willing to give his or her money away.	
41	My son or daughter enjoys responding to the needs of others.	
42	My child administrates tasks, chores and homework well.	
43	My child expresses interest in participating in a missions adventure and/or loves to travel.	
44	My child might seek the opinions of others before making a decision.	
45	My child offers deep and unique insights into Scripture.	
46	My child seeks ways to alleviate people's discomfort.	
47	My child might mention possible ways to aid a person when he or she hears of a need.	
48	My son or daughter displays hope in God when others might doubt.	
49	My child has prayed for someone directly or from afar and seen that person healed.	
50	My child is drawn toward and interested in people of different cultures or ethnicities.	
51	Other children follow my child's lead.	
52	My child cheers others on.	
53	My child displays a servant's heart and nature.	
54	My child is a good listener.	

1=Never   2= Rarely   3=Occasionally   4=Often   5=Always

	Question	Response 1-5
55	My child tends to remember the sick when involved in a family prayer time.	
56	My son or daughter enjoys serving others.	
57	My son or daughter suggests turning to prayer when an opportunity arises.	
58	My son or daughter is willing to pray for a miracle and believe it will happen.	
59	My child is not afraid to strike out in his or her own direction—he or she is not overly clingy.	
60	My child thinks before he or she acts.	
61	My child has prayed for, believed for, and experienced God's provision.	
62	My child is perceptive and discerning.	
63	My son or daughter has faith that God can do miracles.	
64	My son or daughter shares easily with others and might give his or her things away.	
65	When praying, my son or daughter prays more focused and fervently than his or her peers.	
66	My child has concern and compassion for those who are sick.	
67	My child is detail-oriented.	
68	My son or daughter gravitates toward prayer requests that deal with healing.	
69	My son or daughter has shared Scriptures that God has used prophetically in our life or the lives of others.	
70	My son or daughter occasionally speaks truth to me that resonates with my spirit and with God's Word.	
71	My son or daughter is interested in missions and missionaries.	
72	My child has led or attempted to lead friends to Christ.	
73	My child is excited about Scripture and is interested in its nuances and details.	

1=Never   2= Rarely   3=Occasionally   4=Often   5=Always

	Question	Response 1-5
74	When playing with friends, my son or daughter will come up with new ideas for the group and seek buy-in from others.	
75	My child does not rush into new situations before surveying them.	
76	My son or daughter enjoys the task of hospitality.	
77	My son or daughter will say profound spiritual truths beyond his or her years.	
78	My child likes to serve others in partnership as opposed to solitary acts of service.	
79	My child loves greeting people.	
80	My son or daughter helps others respond to life's challenges.	

1=Never   2= Rarely   3=Occasionally   4=Often   5=Always

Scoring the Assessment

In the table below, enter the numerical value from 1 to 5 that you indicated for each question. Add up the four numbers in each row and place the sum in the "total" column. The three highest totals will represent your child's *primary giftings*, while the next three highest totals will represent your son or daughter's *secondary giftings*.

Value for Each Answer							Total	Gift
6		35		42		67			Administration
7		32		62		75			Discernment
4		19		33		52			Encouragement
11		31		36		72			Evangelism
15		16		26		48			Faith
2		10		40		64			Giving
20		55		66		68			Healing
9		13		47		78			Helps
18		22		76		79			Hospitality
1		21		57		65			Intercession/Prayer
23		45		70		77			Knowledge
5		8		51		74			Leadership
3		14		27		46			Mercy
49		58		61		63			Miracles
43		50		59		71			Missions
25		41		54		80			Pastor/Shepherding
12		28		39		69			Prophecy
30		34		53		56			Service
17		24		37		73			Teacher/Teaching
29		38		44		60			Wisdom

Definition of Gifts

Administration: The spiritual gift of *administration* is the ability to manage, plan and orchestrate God's purposes upon the earth.

Apostle: The term "apostle" (Greek, *apostolos*) simply means "a sent one." An apostle is a messenger or an ambassador. The idea is that of representation: An apostle is a personal representative for the one(s) who sent him.

Discernment: The spiritual gift of *discernment* allows the believer to rapidly see to the core of an issue and know the truth. This could relate to doctrinal error, a ministry decision, relational and spiritual issues, and so on.

Encouragement: The spiritual gift of *encouragement* is the ability to strengthen another person through words or perhaps physical presence. Encouragers bring comfort and healing to others. They spur them on.

Evangelism: The spiritual gift of *evangelism* is the ability to boldly share the message of salvation in a way that is clear, concise and effective. Evangelists not only share the gospel but also see people make a decision for Christ.

Faith: The spiritual gift of *faith* is a strong belief in the promises and purposes of God. It is the ability to believe in things that are unseen. Hebrews describes faith as not just believing in things unseen, but also of being sure of those things.

Giving: The spiritual gift of *giving* is the ability to give, with a thankful and cheerful heart, from material resources for the purpose of meeting others' needs or accomplishing some purpose.

Healing: The spiritual gift of *healing* is the ability to be used as a conduit for God to deliver supernatural healing and wholeness to another.

Helps: The gift of *helps* is manifested in believers who invest their talents into the life and ministry of others, allowing the one being served to increase in his or her own abilities.

Hospitality: The spiritual gift of *hospitality* equips believers to provide open arms, open houses and a warm welcome for the purpose of encouragement and equipping.

Intercession/Prayer: The gift of *intercession/prayer* is the ability to pray at length and with effectiveness. Intercessors stand in the gap. In the book of Ezekiel, we see God looking for someone who is willing to stand in the gap (see Ezek. 22:30).

Interpretation of Tongues: *Interpretation of tongues* is the ability to understand and communicate in common language the meaning of a tongue given by another member of the Body of Christ.

Knowledge: The spiritual gift of *knowledge* is twofold. It is the ability to grasp deep scriptural truth and it is also a spiritual insight into particular situations.

Leadership: The spiritual gift of *leadership* is the capability to direct God's people into God's plans. Leaders have the capacity to lead beyond themselves.

Mercy: The spiritual gift of *mercy* starts with a heart for the hurting and the outcast. Mercy shows its fruit in taking action to meet the needs of the hurting and despondent.

Miracles: The spiritual gift of *miracles* is the ability to partner with God to see supernatural power influence the natural order of things.

Missions: The spiritual gift of *missions* is the God-given desire and ability to minister effectively in a foreign culture or subculture.

Pastor/Shepherding: The gift of *pastor/shepherding* is the special ability God gives to certain members of the Body of Christ to assume a long-term personal responsibility for the spiritual welfare of others. Pastors nurture, care for and guide people toward progressive spiritual maturity and becoming like Christ.

Prophecy: The spiritual gift of *prophecy* is the ability to understand God's future purposes and plans for His people.

Serving: The spiritual gift of *serving* is the ability to see a need and use whatever resources are at hand to accomplish the task.

Teacher/Teaching: The spiritual gift of *teaching* is the ability to pass on knowledge and concepts to others in a way they can easily grasp and understand.

Tongues: The gift of *tongues* is the ability to speak in a God-given spiritual language that is for the purpose of edifying the Church or being understood by nonbelievers for the purpose of their salvation.

Wisdom: The spiritual gift of *wisdom* allows a believer to make accurate and well-timed decisions. Wisdom incorporates insight into what is true and right with an understanding of how to implement that knowledge into action.

Scriptural Support for Gifts

1. **Administration:** Exod. 18:13-27; Acts 6:2-4; 1 Cor. 12:28
2. **Apostle:** Acts 14:21-23; 1 Cor. 12:28-29; Eph. 1:1; 4:11
3. **Discernment:** 1 Kings 3:9; Acts 5:3-6; Rom. 12:2; 1 Cor. 2:14; Heb. 5:14; 1 John 4:1
4. **Encouragement:** Acts 4:36; 11:23-24; Rom. 12:8; 1 Thess. 4:18
5. **Evangelism:** Acts 21:8; Eph. 4:11-12; 2 Tim. 4:5
6. **Faith:** Luke 17:5; Rom. 10:17; 1 Cor. 12:9; Phil. 3:9; Heb. 11:1,6
7. **Giving:** Mark 12:43-44; Rom. 12:6,8; 2 Cor. 8:2-3; 9:7
8. **Healing:** Matt. 10:1; Luke 4:40; Acts 3:6-9; 1 Cor. 12:9,30
9. **Helps*:** Acts 6:2-4; 1 Cor. 12:28; 1 Tim. 5:10
10. **Hospitality:** Rom. 12:13; 1 Tim. 3:2; 5:10; Titus 1:8; 1 Pet. 4:9-10
11. **Intercession/Prayer*:** Luke 18:1; John 16:24; Eph. 6:18; 1 Thess. 3:10-13; 5:17; 1 Tim. 2:1-2; 5:5
12. **Interpretation of Tongues:** 1 Cor. 12:10-11,30; 14:5
13. **Knowledge:** John 7:16-17; 17:3; 1 Cor. 12:8; Eph. 3:18-19
14. **Leadership:** Rom. 12:8; Heb. 13:7
15. **Mercy:** Matt. 5:7; Luke 6:36; Rom. 12:8; Titus 3:5
16. **Miracles:** John 20:30-31; Acts 2:22; 19:11; 1 Cor. 12:10
17. **Missions*:** Matt. 28:18-20; Mark 13:10; 16:15; Acts 1:8; 22:21; 1 Cor. 9:19-23
18. **Pastor/Shepherding:** Jer. 23:4; John 10:11; Eph. 4:11-12; 1 Tim. 3:2; Heb. 13:17; 1 Pet. 5:1-4
19. **Prophecy:** Joel 2:28; Rom. 12:6; 1 Cor. 12:10,29; 14:1-3,30-33; Eph. 4:11-12
20. **Serving:** Deut. 10:12; Rom. 12:7; Gal. 6:2; Eph. 3:7; 4:12; 6:7
21. **Teacher/Teaching:** John 7:16; Acts 11:25-26; 13:1; 15:35; Rom. 12:7; 1 Cor. 12:29; Eph. 4:11-12
22. **Tongues:** Acts 2:1-13; 10:44-46; 1 Cor. 12:10-11,28-31; 14:1-5,13-22

23. **Wisdom:** Prov. 3:13; Rom. 11:33; 1 Cor. 12:8; 2 Tim 3:15; Jas. 3:13-18

* Gifts included in the *Discover Your Kid's Spiritual Gifts* spiritual gifts questionnaire but not mentioned in the three key passages of 1 Corinthians 12, Ephesians 4 or Romans 12.

Note: The gifts of Apostle, Tongues and Interpretation of Tongues are not included in the gifts assessment test. The gift of Apostle is a gifting expressed in adult church leadership. The gifts of Tongues and Interpretation of Tongues, if present, are easily discerned.

About the Author

Adam Stadtmiller has been in ministry for more than 15 years, serving in various organizations around the world. He currently ministers at North Coast Calvary Chapel in Carlsbad, California, where he oversees the 30-something ministry. Together, Adam and his wife, Karie, have two daughters, Lily Kate and Lucy Joy.

Adam has a passion for discipleship and launched the Emmaus Center for Discipleship at North Coast Calvary Chapel in 2009. He is also a weekly blogger for conversantlife.com and enjoys endurance sports when not spending time with his family.

If you would like to book Adam for a conference or event, please email him with the dates and details at **adam@giveyourkidsthekeys.com.**

You can also connect with Adam at the following portals:
Facebook: **Adam Stadtmiller**
Twitter: **@adamstadtmiller**
YouTube Channel: **Give Your Kids the Keys**
Websites: **www.giveyourkidsthekeys.com**
www.kidsspiritualgifts.com
Blog: **Adamstadtmiller.com**

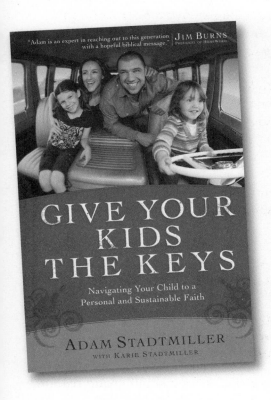

DISCOVER YOUR KID'S SPIRITUAL GIFTS SMALL-GROUP RESOURCE

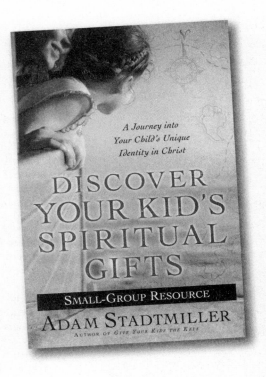

Use *Discover Your Kid's Spiritual Gifts* as a small-group resource for your church. Download a free study guide at:

www.kidsspiritualgifts.com

There you will also find videos from Adam that will help you facilitate your small group. (These are also available at the *Give Your Kids the Keys* YouTube channel.)